Making Technology Work in Schools

Making Technology Work in Schools is an easy-to-use guide for transforming your school into a learner-centered, tech-rich environment. School systems are increasingly adopting ambitious new educational technologies, but how do you make sure they are yielding effective teaching and learning experiences? The authors' proven, intuitive practices speak directly to academic coaches, school technology leads, district technology directors, and teachers on special assignment who are responsible for introducing new tools and programs. After reading this book, you will be able to better prepare the educators you serve to empower their learners, whether digitally savvy or not, to be engaged, collaborative, and better prepared for college and careers.

Timothy D. Green is Professor of Educational Technology and Teacher Education and former Director of Distance Education at California State University, Fullerton, CA, USA.

Loretta C. Donovan is Professor of Educational Technology and Co-Director of the MS in Educational Technology at California State University, Fullerton, CA, USA.

Jody Peerless Green is a teacher on special assignment (TOSA) as an Academic Coach focusing on Educational Technology at La Habra City School District, Orange County, CA, USA.

Other Eye On Education Books Available from Routledge
(www.routledge.com/eyeoneducation)

Integrating Computer Science Across the Core:
Strategies for K-12 Districts
Tom Liam Lynch, Gerald Ardito, and Pam Amendola

Reinventing Crediting for Competency-Based Education:
The Mastery Transcript Consortium Model and Beyond
Jonathan E. Martin

Tech Request: A Guide for Coaching
Educators in the Digital World
Emily L. Davis and Brad Currie

Coding as a Playground: Programming and
Computational Thinking in the Early Childhood Classroom
Marina Umaschi Bers

Universal Design for Learning in the Early Childhood Classroom:
Teaching Children of all Languages, Cultures, and Abilities, Birth – 8 Years
Pamela Brillante and Karen Nemeth

Intentional Innovation: How to Guide Risk-Taking,
Build Creative Capacity, and Lead Change
A. J. Juliani

7 Steps to Sharing Your School's Story on Social Media
Jason Kotch and Edward Cosentino

Making Technology Work in Schools

How PK-12 Educators Can Foster Digital-Age Learning

Timothy D. Green,
Loretta C. Donovan,
and Jody Peerless Green

Routledge
Taylor & Francis Group
NEW YORK AND LONDON

First published 2020
by Routledge
52 Vanderbilt Avenue, New York, NY 10017

and by Routledge
2 Park Square, Milton Park, Abingdon, Oxon, OX14 4RN

Routledge is an imprint of the Taylor & Francis Group, an informa business

© 2020 Taylor & Francis

The right of Timothy D. Green, Loretta C. Donovan, and Jody Peerless Green to be identified as authors of this work has been asserted by them in accordance with sections 77 and 78 of the Copyright, Designs and Patents Act 1988.

Library of Congress Cataloging-in-Publication Data
A catalog record for this title has been requested

ISBN: 978-0-367-02569-4 (hbk)
ISBN: 978-0-367-02570-0 (pbk)
ISBN: 978-0-429-39895-7 (ebk)

Typeset in Optima
by Cenveo® Publisher Services

As trite as it may sound, we dedicate this book to all of the change agents and learners we have worked with over the years. Each has helped shaped who we are and the work we do.

Thank you to my family for being supportive and understanding when I sequestered myself many times to work on this book.

— Tim

There are people who have supported and encouraged me through this book and long before. You know who you are. Thank you!

— Loretta

To my family: your unwavering support and love has been critical throughout this process. I can't thank you enough. I love you!

— Jody

Contents

Foreword

Understandable, Easy to Read, and Useable

We know well that *creating/identifying* promising programs, processes, and practices that could make a difference is easy. There is a plethora of innovations to select from. It's the next phase that is very challenging. *Implementing* a selected program, process, or product is not easy. It takes time, new learning and engaged leadership. There will be "potholes" along the way and the promised outcomes may be slow to materialize. Accomplishing the third phase of a change process, *sustaining*, is seldom systematically planned for, supported, or accomplished.

The track record of achieving successful change with digital innovations most certainly is mixed. Whether it be the introduction of the radio in the "old days," PCs, the web, or social media apps, the extent of implementation ranges widely. There always are wide variations in the "configurations" that are implemented. There also are wide variations in the competence of the users.

One additional challenge with digital innovations is that the innovation itself is constantly changing. The refinements, adaptations, add-ons, and deletions come along rapidly. Any set definition for Fidelity of Implementation is likely to have a very short half-life. The constantly evolving meaning of full implementation raises additional concerns for implementers and for change facilitators. "How can we know for sure when It is fully implemented?"

In other words, from a change science perspective, facilitating implementation of digital innovations presents unique opportunities and challenges. Too often the technology expert delivers the new "box," and assumes that its use is so "obvious" that little support for implementation will be needed. Teachers then have to face Mechanical Level of Use on their own or turn to a colleague who has somewhat deeper expertise. As the "Potholes" accumulate, leaders then have to establish unplanned for implementation supports.

Addressing these opportunities and challenges is the purpose and strengths of this book. The authors are expert in the uses of technology. They are expert in change science. Additionally, they are grounded in today's schools.

"Making Technology Work" is the perfect title for this book. Understanding the opportunities that digital technology represent are foundational to each part and chapters. What is special here is the incorporation of change science models and tools. The three phases of change processes become central to planning and engaging with making technology work in schools.

Another important theme is the authors' "iMakers" construct. We know that today's students bring deep expertise to digital learning. Quite often they will be better ready for introduction of a new technology than will be their teachers. The knowledge and skill students will bring is important to consider in and planning and facilitating change processes. The authors description of iMakers makes sense and helps us understand how better to engage them in new learnings.

You, the reader, will find this book understandable. The organization of the parts and chapters make sense. Some very useful charts and figures are introduced. Their writing style makes the text easy to read. There is a conversational, as well as practical, tone. There are clear explanations of how to plan and facilitate change processes.

This is indeed an understandable, easy to read, and useable resource for making technology work.

Gene E. Hall, PhD
Professor Emeritus, University of Nevada, Las Vegas (UNLV), NV
Research Professor, University of Colorado-Denver (UCD), Denver, CO

Preface

> How can technology help us by opening up the world to deeply engaged learning and worldwide, collaborative problem-solving? In a word, technology, well used, can help us race rapidly to a future that humankind wants and will find fulfilling.
>
> —Michael Fullan (2013, p. 14)

Digital technology is pervasive. It has permeated society and become deeply ensconced in nearly all that we do. It is difficult to go through an entire day without interacting with some form of it. Although the merits of its pervasiveness can be, and are argued (rightly so), we are excited by the opportunities digital technology affords us and our students. We agree with Michael Fullan's sentiment described in the opening quote that technology affords tremendous possibilities if used well. We believe that with increased opportunities, however, comes tremendous pressure—especially for those who are directly responsible for ensuring that digital technology is implemented in equitable and inclusive ways to help improve educational experiences for all students. If you feel this pressure like we do, we are here to help you—starting with our book *Making Technology Work in Schools: How K-12 Specialists Can Foster Digital-Age Learning.*

We are also here to help long after you have finished reading this book. We want to add to your social capital by being part of your personal learning network (or as we like to call it—your purposeful learning network). We'd love to connect with you on social media through Twitter (@theEdTechDoctor, @peerlessgreen, and @CSUF_EdTech) and through Instagram (@peerlessgreen). We encourage you to reach out to us if you have questions, want to share ideas, or simply say hello.

Change Can Be Good

This book is a revamped version of a book we wrote and published in 2014. Our primary goal with that book was to assist school-based change agents (broadly defined) in understanding the change process and how to plan for technology innovation adoption in their school. Examining individual and school readiness for change and technology innovation adoption was a key theme. The primary focus of the book, *Making Change: Creating 21st Century Teaching and Learning Environments* (Donovan & Green, 2014), heavily leaned toward theory rather than practice. We left our readers with the task of determining how best to implement in their school environment the ideas and concepts presented in the book because we did not want to be overly prescriptive. Although the book was well received, what we discovered from reader feedback was that they wanted more direction; they wanted more prescription than we provided. Many of our readers wanted to be guided systematically through a process for facilitating change and innovation adoption. This feedback was the catalyst that led us to write the current book you are reading.

Similar yet Different

Although we have reworked our original book, there remains with our new book a focus on helping readers understand the change process and a focus on learning how to plan for technology innovation adoption in a school setting. What is different is our approach. Rather than leaving readers with the task of determining how best to implement in their school environment the ideas and concepts presented in the book, we provide a more prescriptive process with how to accomplish this. We share our PURPOSE Framework to facilitate this process. Our framework is a systematic approach that was developed based on research-supported practices from educational change theory and innovation adoption **and** from our years of experience in supporting educators, schools, and school districts as they go through the change process to adopt and integrate technology into teaching and learning.

Our primary goal of the book is to help you become capable of facilitating change. In meeting this goal, you will gain the knowledge, skills, and confidence needed to successfully support educators (an entire grade level, a school, or a school district) in their adoption and integration of digital technology in equitable and inclusive ways to improve educational experiences for all students. Points to Consider, Research to Consider, Jody's Perspectives from the Trenches, and step-by-step directions are included throughout the book as scaffolding to support your understanding and implementation of the change process as you apply the PURPOSE Framework in your unique environment. Points to Consider are ideas that we believe change agents should consider as they reflect on the content we present and on their work. Research to Consider are highlights of important research that will help change agents better understand the concepts presented. Jody's Perspective from the Trenches are included to show the PURPOSE Framework in action. These are insights into the work of an educational technology change agent. If you are an academic coach, teacher on special assignment (TOSA), technology lead, district technology director, or for that matter any educator looking for guidance and a gentle nudge in the right direction toward systematically helping educators successfully implement technology in student-centered ways, this book will resonate with you.

The Book Format: The Golden Circle

We've organized the book into three major parts. Each part is made up of multiple chapters. Part I focuses on the *why*, Part II on the *how,* and Part III on the *what*. This structure is based on Simon Sinek's (2009) concept of the Golden Circle described in his book *Start with Why: How Great Leaders Inspire Everyone to Take Action.* Sinek's core message is that you must understand your *why* if you want to achieve exceptional things and inspire others to do the same. Your why, according to Sinek, is your purpose, cause, or belief. Understanding your why is about finding and living your passion. Sinek offers the notion of the Golden Circle to depict the relationship among the why, how, and what. He stated that "A WHY is just a belief. That's all it is. HOWs are the actions you take to realize that belief. And WHATs are the results of those actions—everything you say and do" (p. 67). The why should be at the core of all that we do. Leaders and organizations who have this as their core have achieved a high level of influence because they are at their natural best (p. 38).

Part I begins with a description of our *why*—our core beliefs about technology-rich teaching and learning and why we do what we do as educational technologists and educational change agents. We move into exploring the why of change theory by examining different approaches to educational change to provide you with an overview. Foundational concepts of technology integration and adoption are explored as well. We end with a description of a specific approach to change that is grounded in educational change theory. This approach, the Concerns-Based Adoption Model (CBAM) developed by Gene Hall and Shirley Hord (2020), is one we often use. Our goal with Part I is to provide you with foundational knowledge that leads to understanding how change occurs, how innovations are adopted, and why your role as a change agent in this process is crucial. It will be difficult for you to influence long-lasting and sustainable change and innovation adoption in your school or district without these understandings.

Part II focuses on the *how*—these are the actions we take to live our *why*. It is how we consider the impact we can have on our learners. It is how we view the unique learners in our classrooms. It is how we approach technology and its use for teaching and learning. It is how we consider learning environments. It is how we purposefully select pedagogy and assessments. It is how these elements combine together for our *what*—helping educators adopt and integrate digital technology in equitable and inclusive ways to improve educational experiences for all learners.

There are three major elements that we focus on in Part II: (1) the K-12 learners we have in our classrooms, (2) technology, and (3) instructional practices. The first element begins with a discussion about the impact educators can have on their learners. We then move into describing the characteristics of the K-12 learners we have in our classrooms. In describing these learners, we draw extensively from a chapter we wrote titled, *Learning Anytime, Anywhere through*

Technology: Reconsidering Teaching and Learning for the iMaker Generation (Green & Donovan, 2018). We refer to learners in PK-12 as the iMaker Generation (Green & Donovan, 2018). A description of skills and dispositions these learners need to be competitive in a global economy is also included. Gaining familiarity with the iMakers will prepare you to better serve your learners and the educators who help educate them.

The second element of Part II is our approach to making sense of the deluge of technology options that educators have available. We've written (Green & Donovan, 2018) that over the past decade "The access to and the use of technology in schools for authentic learning has increased exponentially" (p. 17); this access provides unique opportunities for learners to develop skills they need to be true digital age learners. Access alone, however, does not ensure that these opportunities will be effective. Effective learning opportunities are created by educators who have an understanding of the types of technology available and what these technologies are designed to do. We outline and describe an approach to help make sense of the vast options available and to help you select the most appropriate technology that leads to the creation and facilitation of digital age teaching and learning. We end Part II with a discussion on research-based instructional practices that can be infused with technology to provide teaching and learning environments that align with the preferences the iMakers have for engaging in learning.

Part III focuses on the *what*. Our *what*, the result of our *how* (i.e., our actions), is supporting change agents in gaining the knowledge, skills, and confidence needed to successfully support other educators in the adoption and integration of digital technology in student-centered ways. A major element in meeting our what is the PURPOSE Framework. We take a deep dive into our PURPOSE Framework to describe how the framework can be used to cultivate and sustain change needed to foster digital-age teaching and learning. Our goal with Part III is to move step-by-step through the framework to describe how you can be the change agent that brings about sustainable change to an educational environment. Although the change we concentrate on in the book is the use of technology for digital-age teaching and learning, our PURPOSE Framework works with influencing a variety of change.

- Understanding change and innovation adoption
- Embracing change
- Knowing your influence
- Understanding learner needs and wants
- Celebrating differences
- Fostering innovation
- Designing effective learning environments
- Implementing research-supported Instructional practices
- Continuing to learn and grow professionally

To inspire educators to create equitable and inclusive educational experiences for all learners.

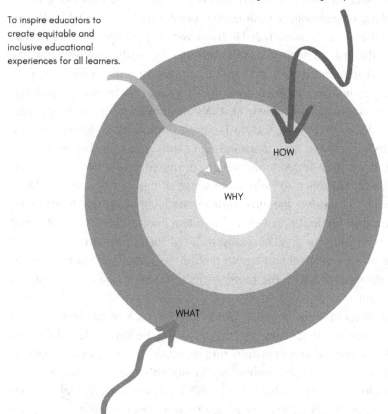

We support change agents in gaining the knowledge, skill, and confidence needed to successfully support other educators (an entire grade level, a school, or a district) in the adoption and integration of digital technology in student-centered ways.

Using the Book

The knowledge and experience you have with facilitating change and innovation adoption should dictate how you approach using this book. Despite our deliberate three-part structure and our belief that every word we've written is indispensable (a bit of a hyperbole, of course), we know that reading it sequentially may not be the most helpful for you. Our suggestion is to begin by reading through the guiding objectives for Parts I and II to determine your comfort level in meeting these. The first two parts of the book, as a reminder, include foundational information needed to successfully use the PURPOSE Framework. If you feel comfortable with the content in Parts I and II, then move on to Part III. You can always come back and refer to the content as needed.

We suspect that most readers will use the PURPOSE framework presented in Part III in its entirety. You may, however, start from whatever point in the framework that makes sense to you based on the specific needs of your educational environment and in what stage of the change process it is. Although the framework is depicted in a linear fashion, it is a recursive and iterative process when implemented. As you apply our framework to your unique educational environment, realize that change is a process, not an event (Hall & Hord, 2020). It will take time to go through the change process. Long-lasting and sustainable change and innovation adoption occur through a systematic and deliberate approach that requires those involved to be patient, open, honest, and reflective. We wish you success as you move through the change process. And remember, we are here to help!

There are a few pedagogical features in the book that we want to point out. We openly admit that we have taken a cue from Hattie and Zierer's book, *10 Mindframes for Visible Learning: Teaching for Success* (a must-read) with our inclusion of specific pedagogical elements based on what they included in their book. We begin each part of the book with learning outcomes that are designed to focus you on the major concepts and ideas that will be presented. This helps bring clarity in what will be presented. We include a self-reflection at the beginning of each part of the book to help activate your prior understandings and experiences. We have included different types of callout boxes throughout the book. These focus on specific points we want to highlight ("Points to Consider"), on important research ("Research to Consider"), and on the concepts and ideas of change in practice ("Jody's Perspective from the Trenches"). We include a summary list at the end of each part to reinforce the major points presented in each part of the book. At the end of each part, we have also included intentional learning opportunities for you to explore and apply the concepts and ideas presented.

From the Trenches

We are excited to have a new member, Jody Green, join the writing team. She provides an important in-the-trenches perspective. As a technology specialist (an academic coach in educational technology) for a Title 1 designated public school district, Jody has been an integral member of the leadership team responsible for bringing about tremendous change in technology access and use to her district. Jody provides first-hand accounts of the work involved in bringing about change and innovation adoption to an educational environment in which access to technology was inconsistent, educator dispositions toward technology use in the classroom was unfavorable at times, and the use of technology, when used, was mostly teacher-centered. Her first-hand experiences will demonstrate the PURPOSE Framework in action.

One Last Thing

Before you dive into the book, we feel it is important to share who we are. We are PK-12 educators. Our experience includes teaching second grade through high school. Tim has taught fourth grade, junior high mathematics and social studies, and high school social studies. Loretta has taught third grade and high school science. Jody has taught English as a Second Language in second to third grade and third to fourth grade combination classes, and she has taught middle school English language arts, mathematics, and social studies. Jody has been teaching in K-12 since 1997, and has been in the same district since 1999. Currently, she is an academic coach in educational technology in her district.

We are also teacher educators. We've taught undergraduates and graduate students in face-to-face and online environments. Currently, Loretta and Tim codirect an online Masters in Educational Technology at California

State University, Fullerton (CSUF) in the Department of Elementary and Bilingual Education (shameless promotion: you can visit our program's site at http://bit.ly/csufedt). Jody has taught as an adjunct for this program. Tim has been working as a Professor at CSUF since 1999, with five of these years as the Director of Distance Education. Loretta has been a Professor at CSUF since 2005.

As professors, we conduct research, write articles and books, and give presentations on educational change, innovation adoption, and the integration of educational technology in teaching and learning in different contexts. We also provide professional development and consulting in PK-12 schools and districts and teacher education programs in the United States and abroad. We maintain a digital presence on the web specifically for this book at http://thepurposeframework.com/. You can find links to resources that support and extend the concepts and ideas we include in the book. You can also find links to other digital resources we maintain and produce.

In addition to being educators, we love dogs, traveling, reading, watching sports, going to see live music, and exercising (well, Jody, and Loretta do).

Acknowledgments

We express our appreciation to everyone at Routledge who had a hand in making this book a reality. We are immensely grateful to Dan Schwartz for supporting us throughout the process and for having a great deal of patience. Thank you, Dan!

The Why of Educational Change and Innovation Adoption

The only constant in life is change.

—Heraclitus

We all are affected by change. Change rarely happens at a time when we are simultaneously ready and able to welcome it. If you have been an educator long enough, you can attest to this. Most educators can regale others with stories about the changes they've been asked to make—curriculum adoptions, revised content standards, benchmark assessments, and last-minute class schedule adjustments. Do these sound familiar? We're certain you could add to this list. As the opening quote stated, change in life is constant, but especially if you are an educator.

We all deal with change differently. No matter what the change is that we are asked to make, how we approach it impacts how effectively we live with it. Helping you effectively approach change—or dare we say learn to embrace it—is our intended outcome of the book. Specifically, we want you to understand the change process as it relates to implementing technology and innovation adoption in your classroom and school. More specifically, we want you to gain the knowledge, skills, and confidence needed to successfully support yourself and other educators in the adoption and integration of digital technology in equitable and inclusive ways to improve educational experiences for all learners. This will help you to be confident in your ability as a change agent. To help you achieve this, we share what we have learned over the past three decades from studying, conducting research, and facilitating change and innovation adoption in educational contexts.

 Point to Consider: You the Change Agent

We believe that every educator is a change agent whether it is in the classroom or whether it is on a larger scale. Although you may not view yourself as a change agent (yet!), it is our intention to help you realize that you are a change agent. You are in a position to help make a positive difference in your environment and the profession. This is why we intentionally use the term change agent throughout the book when we refer to you, the educator reading this book.

The Book Organization

We explain in the Preface that the book is organized into three parts. Part I is the *why*, Part II is the *how*, and Part III is the *what*. This organization scheme is based on the Golden Circle idea that Simon Sinek (2009) describes in his book, *Start With Why: How Great Leaders Inspire Everyone to Take Action*. Sinek's core message is that you must understand your why if you want to achieve exceptional things and inspire others to do the same. Your why, according to Sinek, is your purpose, cause, or belief. Understanding your why is about finding and living your passion. Sinek offers the notion of the Golden Circle to depict the relationship among the why, how, and what. He stated that "A WHY is just a belief. That's all it is. HOWs are the actions you take to realize that belief. And WHATs are the results of those actions—everything you say and do" (p. 67). Your why should be at the core of all that you do. Leaders and organizations who have the why as their core have achieved a high level of influence because they are at their natural best (p. 38).

Part I begins with an explanation of our why—our core beliefs about technology-rich teaching and learning, and why we do what we do as educational technologists and educational change agents. Next, we challenge you to consider your why. This will help you better understand your core beliefs and what motivates your actions as a change agent. We then move into exploring the why of change theory by examining different approaches to educational change to provide you with an overview. Foundational concepts of technology integration and adoption are explored as well. We end Part I with a description of a specific approach to change that is grounded in educational change theory. This approach, the Concerns-Based Adoption Model (CBAM) developed by Gene Hall and Shirley Hord (2020), is one we often use.

Each chapter in Part I focuses on a specific foundational area or concept that will help increase your understanding of educational change and innovation adoption. As you increase your understanding, you will continue moving along the path to becoming a successful change agent. Our primary goal with Part I is to provide you with foundational knowledge that leads to understanding how change occurs, how innovations are adopted, and why your role as a change agent in this process is crucial. It will be difficult for you to influence long-lasting and sustainable change and innovation adoption in your classroom, school, or district without these understandings.

Part I Outcomes

We have outlined five outcomes to guide your reading of Part I. After reading Part I, *The Why of Educational Change and Innovation Adoption*, you will be able to:

1. explain your why;
2. describe the fundamental principles of change theory;
3. comfortably speak with other professionals about the change process;
4. communicate with administrators and educators about challenges associated with the change process and innovation adoption; and
5. provide recommendations on how to approach sustainable innovation adoption.

Self-Reflection

As you read Part I, you will learn that a change agent needs to be aware of the needs of individuals who are being asked to change. This awareness comes about through acknowledging your current comfort level and experiences with initiating and supporting educational change. We've provided a self-reflection exercise for you to assess your comfort level with the concepts presented in Part I. Before you begin reading the chapters in Part I, we suggest that you read the five statements provided and reflect on where you feel you are with the ideas presented in each statement. If you *strongly disagree* with a statement, we suggest that you read the chapter or chapters that focus on that statement. You may need to only skim the chapters in Part I for which you answered *strongly agree* to the statements associated with the chapters.

Assess yourself on the following statements. The self-reflection will help focus your efforts as you engage with concepts and ideas presented in this part of the book.

1 = strongly agree, 3 = neither agree or disagree, 5 = strongly disagree.

1. *I am clearly aware of my beliefs and purpose that drive what I do as a change agent who focuses on educational technology.*

If you rated yourself 3 or below, you will want to make sure you read Chapter 1.

2. *I can discuss with ease the foundational elements associated with educational change.*

If you rated yourself 3 or below, you will want to make sure you read Chapters 2 and 3.

3. *I can clearly define the various important terms and concepts associated with educational change and change theory.*

If you rated yourself 3 or below, you will want to review the list of terms and concepts presented in Chapter 4.

4. *I am thoroughly familiar with different approaches to change and innovation adoption.*

If you rated yourself 3 or below, you will want to make sure you read Chapter 5.

Focusing on the Why

Simon Sinek (2009) described in *Start With Why* that to achieve exceptional things and to inspire others to do the same, you must understand your why. Your why is a belief, a cause, or a purpose that drives what you do. Understanding your why helps you find and live your passion. When you live your passion, it will permeate into all that you do as a change agent. It will help focus your efforts by keeping you grounded in what you believe in.

Gary Keller and Jay Papasan (2013) discuss a similar notion in *The One Thing*. They provide a direct approach on how we can focus our efforts to find our passion that leads to our purpose. They describe a process for understanding how to effectively focus your priorities and efforts on the one thing that will bring about the greatest returns professionally and personally. They indicate that, "Extraordinary results are directly determined by how narrow you can make your focus" (p. 10). This does not mean that we should limit ourselves, other educators, or our learners to small ideas and goals. It means honing in on those activities—based on our passion and priorities—that bring about the greatest results. Those who are high achievers have a clear sense of purpose driven by specific and well-articulated priorities. They are focused on what matters ("the one thing") to achieve the results they desire. Being focused will help inspire others because they will see the passion you have and how it drives what you do. They will want to join you in your efforts to bring about innovation and sustainable change.

Our purpose, which we mentioned in the opening paragraphs, is supporting educators in their adoption and integration of digital technology in equitable and inclusive ways to improve educational experiences for all learners. We approach this through the lens of educational change theory and innovation adoption. This approach helps us make sense of

Point to Consider: Finding Balance—Is It Possible?

An interesting idea discussed in Chapter 8 in *The One Thing* (Keller & Papasan) is balance. Balance is the notion that we are able to attend equally at all times to all elements of our life (e.g., work, family, health). We change agents often beat ourselves up (metaphorically, of course) because we often feel like we are out of balance with our lives due to the work demands placed on us. Keller and Papasan made a bold statement about balance that might make you bristle (or relieved), but one you should take to heart. They state that, "A balanced life is a lie" (p. 73). As a general philosophy, balance is a desirable ideal. Practically, however, it is not realistic. They state that, "Extraordinary results require focused attention and time. Time on one thing means time away from another. This makes balance impossible" (p. 73).

If balance is not possible, how do we make sure that areas of our life do not suffer? Keller and Papasan address this with the idea of counterbalancing. They indicate that there are two types of counterbalancing: "the balancing between work and personal life and the balancing within each" (p. 81). So, why is the discussion of balance important for change agents—especially the notion of not pursuing balance? They sum it up in the following way: "The reason we shouldn't pursue balance is that the magic never happens in the middle; magic happens at the extremes" (p. 76).

If you are a change agent living on the extremes doing extraordinary things (or want to do extraordinary things!), there is no doubt you will feel out of balance at times. Keller and Papasan indicate that this can present tremendous challenges for us. The key is to know how to manage life while living out on the extremes. We suggest reading their book to learn about the strategies they share on how to achieve this.

events, people, and the systems and structures that we work with. Our purpose—our one thing—is woven throughout our teaching, our research, our publications and presentations, and of course, in our work helping lead change and innovation adoption in schools. Our purpose translates into us being passionate about helping educators grow professionally and hone their craft as they use technology in ways that promote high-impact teaching and learning. It also translates into us being passionate about helping change agents gain the knowledge and skills they need to lead change and innovation adoption in schools.

Explaining Your Why

We want you to explore your why. Grab a notebook or some paper (or your favorite digital tool) to write down your ideas. We encourage you to take time right now to answer the following questions and to reflect on your answers. Is there a cause that you are passionate about? What belief or beliefs drive what you do? What do you see as your purpose—your one thing? It is important as a change agent to understand and clearly articulate your why, so you are deliberately and consistently living your passion. This will guide you as you assist others through the change process. It will inspire others to join with you and to take action to innovate and bring about positive change.

 Jody's Perspective From the Trenches: Internal Conflict

It is important to realize that not all change you are asked to make or that you need to help others make will perfectly mesh with your why. There might be instances when you experience some internal conflict. How do you deal with this when you are faced with this type of situation? I do not have a definitive solution because each situation comes with its own set of unique circumstances. I have found, however, that awareness is key. Being aware that conflict can exist will allow you to better cope with the situation. It will allow you to acknowledge your concerns and deal with them. It is important as well to recognize that those being asked to change will have concerns. You will need to address these if the change process is to be a success. Want to know more about this? We discuss this in Chapter 5.

2 | The Why of Educational Change and Innovation Adoption

There are many different approaches to making change. We examine three in Chapter 5 that have greatly influenced our work. It is important to understand that approaches to change vary depending on many elements. One element that directly impacts the change process is where the change is to occur (e.g., an elementary school, a community, a business). Despite the differences among approaches to change, the common element they share is the purpose of bringing about sustainable and long-lasting change. This purpose is the *why* of change.

Another important idea to understand is that the change process is based on years of research and applied practice. There is an entire area of study—Change Theory—devoted to understanding and explaining how individuals and organizations go through change. The genesis of this field is often credited to Kurt Lewin (1947–1980) who was a pioneer in the areas of social, organizational, and applied psychology. Lewin examined change from an organizational perspective through a deliberate exploration of group dynamics and organizational development.

A significant contribution from Lewin is his three-phase process to change. This is a foundation on which other change processes are built. Phase one is *unfreezing*. This phase involves getting rid of the current mindset and resistance to change. The change to be made is introduced. Phase two is *implementation*; this is when change occurs. During this phase, individuals are working through uncertainties about the change. Individuals are at different levels of understanding about the change. Individuals are also at different levels with implementing the change. The final stage is *freezing* (or refreezing). Individuals have a more clear understanding of the change and have adopted the change. The change has become part of what they do. An individual's comfort level often goes back to what it was prior to the change (hence the term, refreezing).

 Point to Consider: Action Research

Action Research is another contribution to educational research Kurt Lewin has been credited with developing. Action Research is a practitioner-based research method that focuses on improving performance and practice. This method has been used frequently in K-12 education as an approach to better understand and address issues that are present in classrooms that affect performance (generally, student learning). An appealing aspect of this research method is the classroom educator as the researcher. This allows the classroom educator to systematically approach critical classroom issues. What is learned through an Action Research study can lead to improved practice of the educator. The insights gained from an Action Research study can also extend beyond the classroom where the study took place. As educators, adding to the knowledge base and helping improve the practice of others is something we should strive to do.

So, how is Action Research conducted? We hesitate to provide an answer to this because we do not want to characterize that Action Research is a simple process. Although the general steps are not difficult to understand, there are many different approaches to Action Research. These approaches are grounded in theoretical frameworks that have nuances that affect how the approaches are carried out. Typically, however, a researcher completes the following steps in an Action Research study: planning, implementation, gathering data about the implementation, and critical reflection. The planning stage involves clearly understanding the issue (i.e., describing what it is, what might be causing it) and determining and developing an intervention or an approach to overcome the issue. Additionally, careful consideration is given as to what data will be gathered to determine the success of the intervention, how the data will be analyzed, and how long the intervention will be implemented. Implementation

---

consists of the intervention put into action. As implementation occurs, data is gathered and analyzed. The final stage is to reflect on the data and the success (or not) of the implementation.

Although we portray the process of Action Research as linear, the process is iterative. If data gathered indicate that the intervention is not having a positive effect on the issue, then the researcher could go back to the planning process to develop another intervention or alter the initial intervention. This new intervention would then be implemented. Data would be gathered, analyzed, and reviewed. Thus, the Action Research process would have gone through a second iteration. It is not uncommon for an Action Research study to go through a few iterations.

We suggest that you take some time to explore the resources on Action Research that are available online. You should explore the resources offered by professional organizations (e.g., ASCD) and higher education institutions, and pay particular attention to how Action Research has been used in educational contexts. We have provided some useful links at the end of Part I. An understanding of Action Research can be helpful in your work as a change agent. It is a tool that you can share with those you work with as an approach to explore performance issues.

A Primer on Educational Change

Educational change is based on fundamental tenets that are important for change agents to understand. We describe four of these major tenets we have gathered from change theorists who have greatly influenced us. It is important to note that the list of tenets we share is not exhaustive; however, what we have included will help you as a change agent while you are engaging in conversations about and trying to stay sane during the change process. Although these tenets may seem obvious once you read them, we feel it is important to discuss what they mean in an educational context.

1. **Change Is a Process.** As change agents, we are well aware that teaching and learning is a complex and multifaceted process that must be carefully planned if it is going to be successful. We must consider such things as the intended learning outcomes, individual student needs, and strategies that will help students meet learning outcomes. The process of change is analogous to the process of teaching and learning. It is complex and multifaceted. As such, we need to carefully plan the change process. In addition, much like student knowledge and skill acquisition not taking place overnight, neither does change. Change, like learning, happens over time rather than because of a one-time event. Hall and Hord (2020, p. 15) suggest that it takes 3–5 years for an innovation to shift from being "an idea" to being a norm. This is an extremely important consideration when taken in the context of K-12 education, where typically an innovation is given 2 years to be adopted and to demonstrate impact. Therefore, as change agents, we must be procedural and systematic in our approach if we are to bring

Jody's Perspective From the Trenches: Change Takes Time

For most change agents, when we learn about something new and get excited about it, we are ready to make a change immediately. This, however, is not true for everyone. I have learned this firsthand through the process of change in my district. Although the innovation of using mobile devices is now thoroughly diffused throughout my work environment, it took 7 years to get to the point where the majority of teachers are consistently using devices in their classrooms. Despite the adoption of devices being fully diffused, we are still working on the mindset shift that comes along with how instruction changes when mobile devices are available in the classroom. It is definitely important to have excitement and to be passionate about an innovation. Do not be disappointed, however, when others do not immediately share your passion, but, at the same time, do not let this discourage you to the point where you lose your excitement and passion. Keep in mind, though your passion may keep you motivated, it may not be enough to motivate others.

about successful and sustained change given the time constraint we are often given.

2. **Change Is Often Initially Discomforting.** We are creatures of habit. We sit at the same table during meetings. We shop at the same stores. We go through the same routines for almost everything we do. These habits make life more predictable, less complicated, and seemingly more manageable. It is not surprising that you might feel some discomfort when you arrive at a meeting and someone is sitting on "your seat" forcing you to sit in a different part of the room. Why do you feel discomfort? Can you explain why you might be upset? Is it the perspective of sitting somewhere new and not having the safety net of knowing the people around you? We often observe educators having a similar reaction of discomfort when they are asked to make changes to their practice. The discomfort is often brought about by uncertainty. There is no way of getting around this—change is always going to bring about discomfort.

The reality, though, is that we always manage to survive change. It may take some longer than others to get over the discomfort, but we all will initially feel some discomfort when asked to change. So, we make it through the meeting sitting in a new location. We eventually find all our groceries despite shopping at a new store. We are able to work out how to get home when our usual road is closed. We survive. The same applies to educational change—we will make the situation work. We survive and often even thrive. A key element to remember as a change agent is that you will experience resistance from those you are asking to change. Do not take this personally. They are experiencing discomfort because they are being asked to do something that is different than what they are used to doing. With your support, their discomfort will fade.

 ## Jody's Perspective From the Trenches: Supporting Discomfort

I have had plenty of experience with change causing great discomfort. When my district first began our process of integrating mobile devices into the classroom, we had a vision that our entire district would be 1:1 with iPads within 3 years. Many teachers were very uncomfortable with the idea that they would have devices in the classroom because they were unsure about the ways in which they would be required to use them. Teachers were required to attend professional learning sessions with me to help them see how mobile devices made exciting educational experiences possible, and even after attending these sessions, often the devices would sit in their charging carts without being used. I was baffled, but I realized that although I believed I had done a great job introducing tools and mindsets that could be used in the classroom, those learning sessions didn't provide enough support to some of our teachers who felt very nervous about this change. In those cases, I made sure to continually reach out to teachers and offer in-class support to help make them feel more comfortable. This approach helped teachers to feel empowered; they realized that they would have support when they took the risk to try something new with their devices.

3. **Change Is Complex and Dynamic.** It is not difficult to observe why change is complex and dynamic when we consider the first two tenets of change that we described above. Now, let's consider some different elements that the process of change includes—people (individuals and groups), culture, space, materials, equipment, resources, and time. When we consider these, it becomes even more clear why change is complex and dynamic. As a change agent, it is important to keep in mind that for every situation where change is to occur, these elements are part of a unique ecosystem. Every ecosystem is influenced by specific complexities of that system. A major complexity is the individuals involved who have different experiences that influence how they engage in the process of change. It is also important to keep in mind that no two change initiatives are identical. Similar to the ecosystem where the change is to occur, the change initiative will have its own unique complexities. The good news is that these complexities can be understood if you take the time to explore them.

 Point to Consider: Understanding the Requested Change

A fundamental mistake often made when engaging in the change process is beginning with an unarticulated or unclear purpose. This can have serious consequences on the success of the process. A clear purpose includes several elements—an explicit description of the change being requested, who is asking for this change to be made, why it is being requested, and who is being asked to change. Understanding these elements helps us manage the complexity and dynamics of the change process. In Part III, we discuss these elements and how you can go about bringing clarity to these elements.

4. **Change Can Be Understood.** Although change is a complex and dynamic process that can initially cause discomfort, if approached in a procedural manner with an open mind, the process of change can be understood. There is a great deal of theory, research, and

best practices that help change agents facilitate the change process. Learning about models and theories of change helps us to understand this process. We discuss several of these models and theories later in Part I.

 ## Jody's Perspective From the Trenches: Theory, Research, and Applied Practice

I find it comforting that the processes I use as a change agent are supported by years of research and applied practice. As I go about my work, I believe it is extremely important to be able to discuss with others the theory and research that supports what I am doing and what I am asking them to do. I have found that this brings about a great deal of credibility and can lead to increased commitment from others about the process. Educational change theory and research is robust. I suggest taking the time to explore this research.

Talking the Talk of Educational Change

Educational change includes an abundance of terms that a change agent should know. Our goal with this chapter is to increase your understanding of educational change by sharing some common terms. Knowing these terms and what they represent will help you better understand the people you work with, your role as a change agent, and what to expect as you help facilitate the change process. We list the terms alphabetically. It is important to note that a term may have other terms from the list included in its description. As an example, in the description of the Adopter Categories we include the term Innovation. It is also important to note that this list is not exhaustive. You will find other key terms within the Points to Consider elements of the book.

Adopter Categories. Everett Rogers (2003) indicated that individuals approach change and the adoption of an innovation with different levels of motivation. He developed five adopter categories for his theory, Diffusion of Innovations. The categories he developed are Innovators, Early Adopters, Early Majority, Late Majority, and Laggards. Innovators are those who are generally open to taking risks. They often need little to no support in adopting an innovation. In many instances, they have already begun using an innovation prior to it being formally introduced into an environment (i.e., their school or district). Think about your school or district. Who is generally the first to try out a new technology? Who is the first to try out a new teaching strategy in their classroom? These individuals will most likely be your Innovators. When facilitating change, you will not need to focus much energy on these individuals. Typically, Early Adopters are careful and judicious when adopting innovations. They are willing to take risks, but will do so only after careful consideration as to how the innovation will impact their practice and their status as an Opinion Leader. Early Adopters are important individuals to identify. They can be helpful in getting others to take risks and adopt an innovation because they often are Opinion Leaders. It is important to note that an Opinion Leader can also crush enthusiasm for an innovation by saying negative things and by not supporting the change process. Spending time and energy on this group early on in the change process is highly important. You want to get them on your side and actively engaged in the change process. The Early Majority are individuals who are slow to take risks. They take significantly longer to adopt an innovation than Early Adopters. They need to see evidence that the innovation works before they are willing to adopt an innovation. Opinion Leaders rarely are part of the early majority. Late Majority individuals approach innovation and the change process with skepticism. They will only consider adopting an innovation after a majority has tried the innovation and it has been adopted by Opinion Leaders. Laggards are not risk takers. They are highly skeptical of change and are likely never to be fully committed to being part of the change and adopting an innovation.

 Point to Consider: Adopter Category Considerations

It is safe to assume that when working with a group of teachers there will be individuals from each adopter category. It is difficult to spend equal time with every teacher. So, what is an effective approach to make sure you maximize your time and resources to make the most impact in helping bring about innovation adoption and positive change? We have found that initially putting the most effort with the Early Adopters brings about the greatest impact. This group, as we've mentioned, is willing to take risks. This group often includes Opinion Leaders who can be champions for using the innovation and influencing others to be on board with going through the change process. Once the innovation begins to be adopted and the change process is well underway, we will focus efforts on the early majority. We spend the least amount of time with the Innovators and the Laggards. The Innovators typically do not need our help and the Laggards will not accept our help, because they are risk aversive and do not want to change.

Change Agent. We use this term throughout the book to describe you, the educator who is instrumental in initiating or supporting (or initiating *and* supporting) change. Change agents can be educators, administrators, parents, students, or anyone who is passionate about taking a direct role in the change process. Everett Rogers (2003; see Chapter 5) defined a change agent "as an individual who influences client's innovation-decisions in a direction deemed desirable by the change agency" (p. 366). Rogers adds that in addition to promoting innovation adoption, a change agent "may also attempt to slow the diffusion process and prevent the adoption of certain innovations with undesirable effects (p. 366). In other words, a change agent is an individual who helps bring about *positive* and *sustainable* change to an organization.

Change Agent (Bottom-Up). A bottom-up change agent is typically an individual teacher (or small groups of teachers) who feels passionate about an innovation he or she has tried and wants to share it with others. Bottom-up change agents are not usually considered an Innovator (see Adopter Categories) or an Opinion Leader (see definition below). Rather, bottom-up change agents are teachers who lead by example. Their passion and genuine desire to share what they have learned and what they are doing in their classroom sparks interest in others to try out the innovation.

Change Agent (Top-Down). A top-down change agent is the person (or individuals) who has mandated that a change occurs, or is the person whose is responsible for ensuring the change occurs. Top-down change agents tend to be school site administrators or administrators at a district office, County Office of Education, or a State Department of Education. School Technology leads can also be considered top-down change agents depending on the role they have during the change process. The top-down change agent's primary responsibilities are to get buy-in from those who are being asked to change and to provide support throughout the entire change process. The support they provide often is in the form of resources (e.g., professional development, technology purchases).

Diffusion Versus Adoption. Rogers (2003) noted that the diffusion of an innovation is different than the adoption of an innovation. This is an important distinction for you to know. Innovation adoption is the process (in stages) that one goes through to adopt an innovation. Innovation diffusion is the process of how an innovation spreads throughout a population (e.g., a school or district) as individuals adopt the innovation.

Gentle Breeze Approach. Rogers (2003) described the approach that many bottom-up change agents take as being a "gentle breeze" approach. With this approach, the bottom-up change agent does not try to force others to adopt the innovation. Rather, the change agent goes about using the innovation and allows others to come to him or her if they want to know more about the innovation or if they want to try it out. As others begin using the innovation and become passionate about it, this often leads to others observing the impact the innovation is making on learning or on the teaching environment. This can lead to additional individuals trying out the innovation. Over time the innovation has spread quietly through a school like a gentle breeze that moves through the branches of trees in a forest.

 # Jody's Perspective From the Trenches: A Gentle Breeze Example

Apple® products are used throughout my district. The first device we introduced was the iPad®. When we first introduced iPads into the classrooms, understandably there was resistance. Teachers wanted to know what the expectations were for using them. Some teachers were uncomfortable with their skill level in being able to use the devices effectively. We provided professional development to help teachers become familiar with the devices and to provide guidance on how to use the devices in the classroom. The professional development (PD) sessions were mandatory—teachers would not be issued the devices until they had attended three sessions. The sessions were well received by teachers; however, the devices were not integrated into the classroom as seamlessly as I had envisioned. My approach to "fix" this included several elements. I offered different PD sessions. I visited a school each week to offer a lunch-time session to work with teachers. I sent out an e-mail blast every 2 weeks with technology integration tips. Although these elements were helpful, it was not until I took a less formal approach that I began to see increased use of the iPads and interest in using them in more student-centered ways. Rather than scheduling formal PD and other events, I let teachers know I was available to come into their classroom to observe, plan, and co-teach. When I visited schools, I informally shared ideas with teachers. I asked what they needed support with, and I offered to do demonstration lessons to model instructional uses of the iPads. I have found that being available for this type of support created what Rogers called a "gentle breeze" for bringing about change. Change was taking place slowly but surely. I began to observe more teachers using the iPads. More teachers heard what I was offering. As a result, the number of teachers who wanted my support increased. I was invited into more classrooms to co-teach and to conduct demonstration lessons. Though I continue to offer formal professional development and other opportunities. I have realized that a less formal approach is crucial. Teachers will seek support when they are ready; often, this happens after they have seen and heard what you have done with and for their peers.

Innovation. In *Diffusion of Innovations*, Rogers (2003) defines an innovation as "an idea, practice or object that is perceived as new by an individual or other unit of adoption" (p. 12). He adds that newness is a relative term and what may be considered an innovation for an individual may not be new or an innovation for someone else. Michael Fullan (2016) reinforces this notion by describing an innovation as the specific content of a new program. Gene Hall and Shirley Hord (2020) suggest that an innovation can be a product such as curriculum or a process such as a pedagogical approach. We use the term innovation to describe a combination of both product and process such as the changed pedagogy that comes with the addition of new technology in a school or a classroom. We want to be very clear that we distinguish innovation from innovativeness. Fullan (2016) makes this distinction by describing innovativeness as "the capacities of an organization to engage in continuous and new improvement" (p. 10). Without a culture of innovativeness, however, no innovation adoption will be sustained.

Innovation Adoption. Not surprisingly, innovation adoption is the process of adopting a new product or process such as a coding curriculum or a behavioral intervention program. What we consider to be most important to understand when discussing innovation adoption is that the way an innovation is adopted is always unique. Additionally, it is important to keep in mind that the rate of innovation adoption for individuals is always variable. Rogers (2003) attributes this to what he calls the perceived attributes of innovations (p. 15). Some individuals will adopt the innovation into their practice quickly while others may never fully adopt it. We discuss this idea in more depth in Chapter 5.

 Point to Consider: Once an Innovator, Not Always an Innovator

It is extremely important to note that someone is not necessarily always an Innovator. Tim, for example, is an innovator when it comes to trying tools or types of tools (e.g., augmented reality, virtual reality) that can be used in online teaching and learning. He frequently uses tools when they first come out. However, he would not be considered an Innovator when it comes to smartphones despite his willingness to try out emerging tools in other contexts. Additionally, although he has an affinity for Apple products, he is typically a generation or two behind the latest version of the iPhone. He waits to read reviews about the phone and determine how the phone has worked for others before he upgrades. As you work with others, it is important to keep in mind that once an innovator does not mean always an innovator. It will save you some grief if you keep this in mind.

Intervention Mushrooms. Hall and Hord (2020) state that it is important to identify early in the change process those individuals who they refer to as Intervention Mushrooms. Intervention Mushrooms are identified by Hall and Hord as poisonous or nutritious (p. 228). A poisonous mushroom is someone who is highly resistant to change, and like an Opinion Leader (as Rogers described) can influence how others feel about an innovation and about being asked to change. However, unlike Opinion Leaders, they do not help you promote the adoption of the innovation; they do the opposite. Poisonous mushrooms may be highly vocal in their discontent or may even simply refuse to use the innovation. A nutritious mushroom is the opposite. This is often someone whose enthusiasm for the innovation is contagious. You should identify nutritious and poisonous mushrooms early in the change process and include them as much as possible. For poisonous mushrooms, try to determine what it is that they have potentially misinterpreted about the innovation. Provide them with information to bring clarity about the change being requested and to clear up their misunderstanding. It is important to keep in mind the fundamental tenet that change is initially uncomfortable. Be aware that the negativity may be stemming from a place of insecurity about having to change. For nutritious mushrooms, you will want to include them to get their assistance in promoting the innovation.

Laggard. A Laggard, as you might expect, is a person who lags behind. In the case of the change process and innovation adoption, Laggards are those who are the last to adopt an innovation, if they adopt at all. When they do adopt, it is typically because they are left with no other option. Rogers (2003), in describing categories of adopters, equates the Laggards to traditionalists. He adds that they are usually wary of change agents. What this means for you as a change agent is that you will need to take a unique approach with these individuals. Part III of the book includes strategies for working with Laggards.

One-Legged Interview. One-legged interviews are quick, informal conversations that take place as you pass through the hallways. According to Hall and Hord (2020), the focus of these conversations is on how things are going. As a change agent, you can gain a great deal of information from these unplanned conversations. Hall and Hord share that research indicates that one-legged interviews can have a positive impact on teacher acceptance of change (p. 21). Make sure you pay attention to body language and gestures in addition to the words that are spoken. Eye rolls, thumbs-up, or smiles can help you gain insight into how the innovation adoption process is proceeding. What you gain from these conversations can help guide the support you need to provide.

Opinion Leaders. Opinion Leaders, a phrase coined by Rogers (2003) describes those who have a great deal of sway on their peers. As a result, their peers often follow what the Opinion Leaders do. The followers will often say, "Well if he can do it, I can probably do it too." This is not because the followers feel superior to the Opinion Leader—it is because the Opinion Leader is an individual to whom the followers can relate. Often, an Opinion Leader is not the most tech-savvy person who tries new things; rather, Opinion Leaders are usually the individuals who are willing to take the risk to try something new. Opinion Leaders play a key role in the innovation-adoption process. As a change agent, it is extremely important for you to identify the Opinion Leaders and work with them closely.

Phases of Adoption. Michael Fullan (2007) indicates that there is a dynamic relationship that exists between the key phases of innovation adoption. The phases work together in a complex process. Fullan labeled the three phases of his model as initiation, implementation, and institutionalization. The **initiation** phase of innovation adoption is where decisions are made and plans are established prior to introducing something new (i.e., the innovation) into the environment (e.g., the classroom, the school, the district). This phase can be impacted by the characteristics of the innovation (i.e., complexity, accessibility), readiness of the individuals who are being asked to adopt it, and the relationship between this readiness and the innovation (i.e., familiarity, similarity to existing practices or equipment). The next phase is **implementation**. This phase is when individuals start using the innovation. According to Fullan, characteristics that impact the implementation phase can be categorized into characteristics of change (need, clarity, complexity, practicality), local characteristics (district, community, principal, teachers), and external factors (policy and government). One of the most important things to remember about the implementation phase is how the innovation gets implemented. It is not always consistent. The final stage, **institutionalization**, is when the innovation has become part of everyday activity. During this phase, some are already starting to think about how to modify and expand the way the innovation is being used. Additionally, most if not all are implementing the innovation and professional development is no longer needed (unless there are new teachers or others not familiar with the innovation). At this point, resources are being used on finding ways to sustain the use of the innovation.

5 | Different Perspectives on Change

It is important to understand that there are many perspectives on change. We have been decidedly influenced by three perspective—Everett Rogers, Michael Fullan, and Gene Hall and Shirley Hord. They are among the most well-known experts in Educational Change and Innovation Adoption. Their perspectives are research-based and have been used for many years to guide research (including our own) related to innovation adoption and educational change. You should aim to understand the contributions of these individuals as they provide the main foundation for the why of educational change.

The perspectives of Rogers, Fullan, and Hall and Hord have been woven throughout this book. Despite their uniqueness, these perspectives are not completely dissimilar. They all point to the need to consider and to address a collection of interrelated factors if an innovation is going to be adopted and diffused, and if the change is to be sustained. Part III is based on these three perspectives and will guide you through the innovation adoption and change process. The process we share is our PURPOSE Framework. You will be able to use this framework to help you address the uniqueness of your context and the change you are responsible for helping facilitate.

Everett Rogers (1931–2004) is most well-known for his work on innovation adoption and the diffusion of innovations. His book, *Diffusion of Innovations*, is seminal work in these areas. Although Rogers was a social scientist whose initial research in the early 1960s focused on the agriculture sector in the United States and the social change that occurred among farmers, his perspective on change is highly applicable to educational contexts. The foundational idea of diffusion of innovations is that when asking individuals to go through the change process and adopt an innovation, we should seek to understand change from the perspective of the individual being asked to change.

Rogers described that individuals go through stages in the innovation adoption process. These stages are knowledge, persuasion, decision, implementation, and confirmation. The **knowledge stage** is when an individual is first exposed to an innovation. The individual lacks enough information about the innovation to do anything meaningful with the innovation. At this point, the individual will most likely not have much interest or excitement about the innovation. The **persuasion stage** is when an individual becomes interested in the innovation and actively engages in finding out information about the innovation. Once an individual has the information needed to understand the innovation, they move into the **decision phase**. This phase is when an individual weighs the strengths and weaknesses of using the innovation. The individual will use this information to either reject or adopt the innovation. If an individual decides to adopt an innovation, the **implementation phase** is next. The individual will use the innovation based on the individual's needs. During this stage, the individual is determining how useful the innovation is to them. The individual may search for additional information about the innovation to gain a better understanding of it. The final phase, **confirmation**, is when an individual decides to continue to use the innovation. The individual will consider whether adopting the innovation was an appropriate decision for the individual and for the organization.

 Point to Consider: Rate of Adoption

It is important to keep in mind that individuals adopt an innovation at different rates. This cannot be avoided even though the individuals may be at the same school, have gone through the same professional development, and was provided similar support. It is important as well, as a change agent, for you to constantly remind yourself of this because it will help you to be patient, plan differentiated professional development, provide unique levels of support, and be realistic in tracking the progress of your efforts.

Rogers suggests that a series of questions should be used during the Initiation Phase to help bring about a clear understanding of the innovation. These questions are helpful for those being asked to change and for change agents who are leading the change process. The questions relate to the characteristics of the innovation. These characteristics are listed in parenthesis after each question.

1. Is the innovation better than what we are using currently? (Relative advantage)

2. Is this innovation consistent with my values, experiences, and needs? (Compatibility)

3. Is this innovation going to be hard for me to understand and use? (Complexity)

4. Can I just use this innovation on a trial basis and then decide? (Trialability)

5. Will others be able to tell that things have changed and improved? (Observability)

Answers to these questions are helpful in determining how ready an individual is to accept the change he or she is being asked to make. They can help us anticipate to what degree an individual will adopt the innovation associated with this change. We do not necessarily have individuals ask these questions before adopting an innovation. We find that individuals will naturally consider these characteristics about an innovation (and answers these questions or ones like these). We use these questions as a starting point to consider how the individuals we are working with will react to the innovation and the change process. Considering these questions allows us to plan accordingly for the change process and make informed decisions about the level of information and type of scaffolding we need to provide.

Michael Fullan is a former Dean of the Ontario Institute for Studies in Education at the University of Toronto. At the writing of this book, he is the Global Leadership Director for a global organization that is an authority on educational reform. Of his many publications, the one we use as a foundation for our work is *The New Meaning of Educational Change* (2016). Fullan, like other change theorists, suggests that change is a process. He describes change occurring at an individual level and at the institutional level.

Fullan considers change from a subjective perspective and an objective perspective. In discussing the subjective meaning of change, Fullan indicates to carefully consider the teacher and to acknowledge the endless list of tasks, decisions, and behaviors they experience each day. Fullan provides a caution about expecting all individuals to accept and implement an innovation in the same way (which is a similar notion to Hall and Hord's (2020) rationale for their Innovation Configuration [IC] Map [IC Map]). Fullan also reminds us that individuals, in particular educators, need to find meaning and value in what they are being asked to do before they will actually do it. In contrast to the subjective meaning of change, Fullan presents the objective reality of educational change. Although he considers the subjective meaning to be somewhat easy to describe because we can isolate different factors, Fullan suggests that the objective reality is far more complex and multidimensional (p. 27). It is the complexity that we must always consider when applying change theory.

Fullan identifies three main dimensions (p. 28) for applying the objective perspective of change when initiating and implementing change. First, we need to consider what most people refer to as the innovation—the content of the innovation (e.g., curriculum, technology, new standards). We can think of this as a physical dimension. In addition to this dimension, we then need to be aware of new pedagogy associated with the content of the innovation. This could be considered an action dimension. We also need to remember the beliefs (personal dimension) the individuals have regarding the innovation and associated new pedagogies. This may seem straightforward; however, Fullan warns us about potential difficulties that can impact the innovation adoption process. Primarily, Fullan discusses the potential for having a surface-level change in which people seem to embrace and implement (action dimension) the innovation (physical dimension), but in reality they have not internalized the process (personal dimension). This will most likely result in the innovation adoption not being sustained. Essentially, without teacher commitment, change will be short-lived.

Gene Hall and Shirley Hord have written numerous books to help people understand educational change. Their work has been used to understand, implement, and research change in educational contexts. Hall and Hord developed the Concerns-Based Adoption Model (CBAM, pronounced see-bam) to provide a systematic approach to facilitating change. The CBAM consists of three major constructs: the Stages of Concern (SoC), ICs, and Levels of Use (LoU).

Research to Consider: CBAM Stages of Concern Research

We have used CBAM quite frequently in our work. Most recently, we have used IC in our work with one-to-one programs at the middle school level (Donovan, Green, & Hartley, 2010) and with describing K-8, 21st-century learning environments (Donovan, Green, & Mason, 2014), as well as SoC to examine technology integration in a teacher education program (Donovan & Green, 2010). We have provided the citations if you are interested in exploring the studies.

Donovan, L., & Green, T. (2010). One-to-one computing in teacher education: Faculty concerns and implications for teacher educators. *Journal of Digital Learning in Teacher Education (formerly JCTE)*, 26(4), 140–148.

Donovan, L., Green, T., & Hartley, K. (2010). An examination of one-to-one computing in the middle school: Does increased access bring about increased student engagement? *Journal of Educational Computing Research*, 42(4), 423–441.

Donovan, L., Green, T., & Mason, C. (2014). Examining the 21st century classroom: Developing an Innovation Configuration Map. *Journal of Educational Computing Research*, 50(2), 161–178.

When planning for change, Hall and Hord suggest that change agents start by determining the concerns of the individuals being asked to change before the change agents make decisions about how best to approach the change process. The **SoC** construct of CBAM assists in determining concerns. The SoC includes two components: the Stages of Concern Questionnaire (SoCQ) and one-legged interviews (see Part I, Chapter 3). The questionnaire is a 35-item survey that asks a range of questions about an individual's perception of the innovation they are being asked to adopt, as well as how they feel about the innovation adoption. The results of the survey are presented as a Concerns Profile. The Concerns Profile helps change agents understand the degree with which the group as a whole are ready to adopt the innovation. The Concerns Profile is represented as a continuum. At one end of the continuum is Self Concerns that indicate an individual (or group) is aware of what is going on but wants and needs more information. The opposite end of the continuum is the Impact Concerns that indicate an individual is fully immersed in using the innovation and is considering what is next (e.g., how to improve the innovation). In the middle of the continuum are the Task Concerns that highlight concerns related to the on-going use and management of the innovation.

Although Hall and Hord recommend a profile for the group based on the results of the SoCQ, we generally examine subgroups (e.g., grade levels, teachers, administrators, years of experience) as well. If you are surveying large groups, however, the time involved in doing this can be prohibitive. Using the individual profiles, together with a working knowledge of the environment (some of which is gathered through one-legged interviews), assists in identifying Opinion Leaders, nonusers (Laggards), and people who won't need as much support (Innovators). The group and individual profiles fit together to help change agents make decisions about the types and amount of support, professional development, and mentoring that is needed to help increase the adoption of the innovation and its diffusion throughout the environment.

 ## Point to Consider: Thinking Back to the Tenets of Change Theory

As you reflect on the three constructs of CBAM, it is important to know that these constructs tie directly to the four tenets of Change Theory we explored in Chapter 3. The data gathered through the SoCQ, the development of IC Maps, and the LoU assessment will help remind change agents that change is a process (tenet 1), that individuals experience discomfort when going through during the change process (tenet 2), and that the change process is complex and dynamic (tenet 3).

IC is a process that helps change agents determine what the implementation of the innovation looks like once the innovation has been adopted. The process of IC focuses on the collection of data about the ways the innovation is being implemented. This data is used to create an IC Map describing these ranges of implementation. Essentially, an IC Map is a series of descriptions of all the configurations that an innovation is being adopted in an environment where the change process is occurring. It is important to know that it is not unusual, in fact it is more common than not, to observe an innovation being used differently—multiple configurations—at the same school. It is also important to understand that a specific configuration could be a blend of what is occurring in different classrooms. Finally, a configuration may not be the same for each class period for the same teacher. The role of the IC Map is not to place judgment on the different ways an innovation is being adopted. Instead, it should be used to make informed decisions about the next steps in the change process.

 ## Point to Consider: Innovation Configurations Example

In our own research (Donovan, Green, & Mason, 2014), we created an IC Map of a 21st-century teaching and learning environment in which all students had 1:1 laptop–computer access. In this study, the innovation was the 21st-century skills of creativity, critical thinking, communication, and collaboration. We found two configurations—content-based learning and project-based learning—both of which promoted 21st-century skills in students. Although distinct in their own ways, the two configurations had common elements as well, specifically the school ecology (culture, programs, and community). Based on this information, we were able to make recommendations to others interested in promoting 21st-century skills and to the school about specific foci for professional development for different groups of educators at the school.

The third construct of CBAM is the **LoU**. Hall and Hord (2020) developed the LoU construct of CBAM to provide greater distinction between simply stating a person is a nonuser or a user of an innovation. The LoU construct acknowledges that use and nonuse are not a dichotomy (p. 135), rather a user or nonuser have different approaches to use. Although seemingly similar to SoC that looks at reactions to innovation adoption, LoU looks at behaviors associated with use or no use (p. 135).

There are eight levels or behavioral profiles within the LoU framework. Nonusers exhibit different levels of nonuse ranging from nonuse at all to information seeking to preparing to use. Users, on the other hand, can be using or implementing an innovation in five different ways—mechanical use, routine use, refinement, integration, and renewal (Hall & Hord, 2020, p. 137). To determine LoU, a similar process as the SoC is used that includes one-legged interviews and long-term data collection. Similar to the other two CBAM constructs, LoU data analysis is complex. A LoU evaluation can assist the change agent in planning, supporting users and nonusers, and making informed judgments about the degree to which the innovation is addressing the need it was intended to address.

 Key Points From Part I: The Why of Educational Change and Innovation Adoption

Let's Review!

- Every educator is a change agent.
- You must understand your why—your beliefs, your purpose—if you are to be an effective change agent who is able to inspire others. (Chapter 1)
- Change has a theoretical and research foundation. (Chapter 2)
- Educational Change is a systematic process for improving teaching and learning. (Chapter 2)
- There are tenets of change that are important to understand. (Chapter 3)
- There is a vocabulary associated with change. (Chapter 4)
- There are multiple perspectives on change. (Chapter 5)

 Let's Explore and Practice

Now that you've made it through Part I, it is time to explore and practice with the concepts and ideas we included. We have provided a few activities that can help you delve into theses.

1. Review why we consider all educators to be change agents. How would you explain this idea to a colleague?

2. We described that Simon Sinek's concept of the Golden Circle influenced how we organized the book. What three elements make up the Golden Circle? How do these three elements work together? How can you use this idea to hone in on what you do as a change agent?

3. Your *why* is your beliefs and purpose. It is the passion that drives what you do. As a change agent, it is important to be able to clearly describe your why. We encourage you to take some time to think about and reflect on your why. Write it down. Illustrate it. Share it with someone who you trust will give you convivial but honest feedback. Send it to us. We'd love to read it and give feedback.

4. We discussed finding balance as a change agent. What are the main ideas you took from this discussion? What important points might you pass along to other change agents that you believe they would find helpful?

5. We shared four tenets of educational change. Develop a slide deck with four slides—one tenet per slide. Use no more than one image and 15 words on each slide to explain each tenet. When you are done, you will have the start of a presentation that you can use to explain educational change.

6. Consider specific examples from your own experiences or ones in your school environment that illustrate the four tenets. Add these to the slide deck you created.

7. We discussed adopter categories. Think about the latest technology that educators were asked to adopt at a school you worked with or at your school. Who were the opinion leaders? Who were the Early Adopters? Did you have innovators already using the technology? Who were the laggards?

8. Consider the terms we shared throughout Part I. Develop an info-graphic to share with colleagues that explains what you believe are the most important or difficult terms.

9. Three different approaches to educational change and innovation adoption were presented. Create a nonlinguistic representation that depicts the similarities that the three approaches share.

10. We discussed the concept of action research. Describe how action research can assist you as a change agent.

Digging Deeper into Educational Change and Innovation Adoption

We've provided some resources that you can explore if you would like to dig deeper into educational change and innovation adoption. The resources are websites, books, and articles that we have found helpful in our understanding, development, and growth as change agents.

- "What Is Action Research?" book chapter from the Association for Supervision and Curriculum Development (ASCD). http://www.ascd.org/publications/books/100047/chapters/What-Is-Action-Research%C2%A2.aspx

- "Overview of the Action Research Process" book chapter from Corwin Press. https://www.corwin.com/sites/default/files/upm-binaries/23146_Chapter_2.pdf

- *Themes in Education: Action Research*, a book written by Eileen Ferrance available at https://www.brown.edu/academics/education-alliance/sites/brown.edu.academics.education-alliance/files/publications/act_research.pdf

- Overview of CBAM. https://www.air.org/resource/concerns-based-adoption-model-cbam

- ASCD, a professional learning and community for educators. http://www.ascd.org/Default.aspx

- Michael Fullan's website with many resources about educational change. https://michaelfullan.ca/

- Everett Rogers: presentation on diffusion of innovations (begins at minute 7). https://www.youtube.com/watch?v=j1uc7yZH6eU

II

The How of Educational Change and Innovation Adoption: Learners, Technology, and Instructional Practices

If you can tune into your purpose and really align with it, setting goals so that your vision is an expression of that purpose, then life flows much more easily.
—Jack Canfield

The *why* of educational change was explored in Part I. We began by having you consider your why—your beliefs and purpose as a change agent who focuses on educational technology and who helps others go through the process of change and innovation adoption. We discussed foundational concepts of change that included four major tenets of change. We provided three approaches to change and innovation adoption that have influenced our thinking and the work we do. In addition to these ideas, we shared that our purpose (our why) is the integration of digital technology in equitable and inclusive ways to improve educational experiences for all learners. This leads us to the design and implementation of learner-centered educational environments in which learning occurs anytime, anywhere through technology (Green & Donovan, 2018). We also shared that our *why* manifests into our *what* of helping change agents gain the knowledge and skills they need to lead change and innovation adoption in schools (the primary out-come of this book). We provide support for change agents as they design and implement student-centered teaching and learning that is equitable and inclusive for all learners. We described that we approach our purpose through the lens of educational change and innovation adoption, which helps us make sense of events, people, and the systems and structures that we work with.

The focus of Part II shifts to *how*. Simon Sinek (2009) indicated that your how is the actions you take to realize your why—your purpose. As we consider our actions as change agents, we find it useful to organize them into categories based on the complexities of teaching and learning. We educators are intensely aware of how complex teaching and learning is and that there are many elements we need to be experts in and we deal with these elements every school day. We need to be masters at attending to all of these—often simultaneously—if we are to maximize learning for our learners. When considering this proposition, it is not difficult to com-prehend how overwhelmed our colleagues can get when they are asked to make a change and include one more element into their practice. You must take this into consideration when you are working with them. You will be prepared to handle this if you are keenly aware of your how.

Learners, technology, and instructional practices are the three catego-ries we use to organize and consider our *how*. We use these categories because they are the major components of teaching and learning that we change agents can influence the most. The chapters in Part II are organized around these components. We begin Part II by describing two concepts that are important for you to understand as a change agent: teaching and learning as an ecology and collective teacher efficacy. These concepts have shaped our approach to being change agents. After these two concepts, we move into examining the characteristics and dispositions of the learners we have in our classrooms. We call these learners the iMakers (Green & Donovan, 2018). It is crucial to have a solid understanding of their gen-eral characteristics and dispositions if we are to best meet their learning needs. We discuss how they prefer to engage in learning. We discuss the contemporary skills that they need to be effective in and outside of school. We also discuss the tools they have access to and how they use these tools. Technology is explored next. We share our framework for making sense of the range of technologies that are available for use in teaching and learning. We explain our approach for staying (or attempting to stay) current with technology. We end Part II with an examination of instructional practices. We discuss 10 research-based instructional practices that can be used in the design of effective teaching and learning environments for the *iMakers*.

Although we understand that your how will be different than ours, we share our how because we believe our how will provide you with foundational ideas to consider as a change agent. We believe that sharing our how can help you reflect on yours. Additionally, we believe our approach to categorizing our how is one that you could follow as a change agent if you are struggling to determine your own approach.

Self-Reflection

As you read Part II, you will learn that a change agent needs to be aware of numerous elements that impact teaching and learning. This awareness will come about through acknowledging your current comfort level and experiences with these elements: learners, technology, and instructional practices. We've provided a self-reflection exercise for you to assess your comfort level with the concepts presented in Part II. Before you begin reading the chapters in Part II, we suggest that you read the 10 statements provided and reflect on where you feel you are with the ideas presented in each statement. If you *strongly disagree* with a statement, we suggest that you read the chapter or chapters that focus on that statement. You may need to only skim the chapters in Part II for which you answered *strongly agree* to the statements associated with the chapters.

Assess yourself on the following statements. The self-reflection will help focus your efforts as you engage with the concepts and ideas presented in Part II of the book.

1 = strongly disagree, 3 = neither agree or disagree, 5 = strongly agree.

1. *I am very good at selecting elements that lead to the development of effective learning environments for my learners.*

If you rated yourself 3 or below, you will want to focus on Chapter 6.

2. *I am clearly aware of how my perceptions of my students' abilities have on their achievement.*

If you rated yourself 3 or below, you will want to focus on Chapter 7.

3. *I can accurately describe to my colleagues the impact that collective teacher efficacy has on student achievement.*

If you rated yourself 3 or below, you will want to focus on Chapter 7.

4. *I can clearly describe the characteristics that make up the learners in my classroom.*

If you rated yourself 3 or below, you will want to focus on Chapter 8.

5. *I am confident in my ability is to use technology in ways that engage learners and positively impact their learning.*

If you rated yourself 3 or below, you will want to focus on Chapter 9.

6. *I can easily select technology tools that assist my learners in developing soft-skills (e.g., critical thinking, creativity).*

If you rated yourself 3 or below, you will want to focus on Chapter 9.

7. *I am thoroughly convinced that I can describe the rationale (the why) behind each technology tool I use with learners.*

If you rated yourself at a 3 or below, you will want to focus on Chapter 9.

8. *I know perfectly well how to stay current on the latest trends and issues with educational technology.*

If you rated yourself 3 or below, you will want to focus on Chapter 9.

9. *I am extremely capable of discussing effective pedagogical approaches that leverage technology to positively impact student achievement.*

If you rated yourself 3 or below, you will want to focus on Chapter 10.

10. *I am highly capable of helping my colleagues create teaching and learning that effectively integrates technology to support student learning.*

If you rated yourself 3 or below, you will want to focus on Chapters 9 and 10.

Part II Outcomes

We have outlined eight outcomes to guide your reading of Part II. After reading Part II, *The How of Educational Change and Innovation Adoption: Learners, Technology, and Instructional Practices*, you will be able to:

1. describe how teacher self-efficacy and collective teacher efficacy affects learners;

2. explain how teaching and learning is like an ecosystem;

3. define the major characteristics of the iMaker Generation;

4. describe how iMakers prefer to engage in learning, particularly using technology;

5. explain how technology can be used with learners to develop critical thinking, creativity, and effective communication and collaboration skills;

6. explain what learning anytime, anywhere through technology is;

7. describe the major elements of different research-based instructional practices that align with the learning preferences of iMakers; and

8. implement a plan for keeping current with educational technology trends and issues.

An Ecological Perspective on Teaching and Learning

The statement you read in the next sentence will not surprise you. Teaching and learning includes many components. We feel slightly silly having stated this because as a change agent this will seem obvious. However, we believe this statement leads to an important concept that is crucial for change agents to keep in mind when working through the change process. The interconnected components make teaching and learning a complex process. These components influence what takes place in the classroom in ways that we may not immediately understand or often consider. It is important to realize that change with one component may cause an unexpected consequence.

We know that the more you understand about these components and how they are interconnected, the better equipped you will be as a change agent to handle the components effectively and help others to do the same. This understanding will help you develop the mindset of being a careful observer of what is happening in the environments where you work. You will be able to determine what is causing something to occur, which will allow you to approach it effectively to influence long-lasting, positive change.

Our approach is to take an ecological perspective as we make sense of the many interconnected components that make up teaching and learning. With this perspective, we consider a classroom (or a school or district) as an ecosystem with its many interconnected parts. Our mindset is to examine the multiple components of the ecosystem—particularly the components of learners, educators, technology, and instructional practices—as we "examine how they combine to make up the environment, influence how it operates, and affect learning" (Green & Donovan, 2018, p. 225). An ecological perspective encourages us to take a holistic view rather than a narrow view when approaching change and innovation adoption. It is important to consider change and technology adoption in context rather than as an isolated event if we want the adoption to be sustained. The more you know about the context, the more likely you will be able to attend to components that lead to issues affecting the change process and technology adoption.

 Research to Consider: Ecological Perspective and Technology

Our ecological perspective has been influenced by the research of Zhao and Frank (2003) described in their article *Factors Affecting Technology Uses in Schools: An Ecological Perspective*. They discussed the notion of considering technology adoption in context rather than as isolated events. They suggested that the introduction of technology into a learning environment can be compared to the introduction of a new species into an ecosystem. We believe this is a must-read article to gain a clear understanding of the disruption technology can have when introduced into a teaching and learning ecosystem.

Zhao, Y., & Frank, K. A. (2003). Factors affecting technology uses in schools: An ecological perspective. *American Educational Research Journal, 40*(4), 807–840.

7 | Teacher Self-Efficacy and Collective Teacher Efficacy

Albert Bandura (1977) developed the theory of self-efficacy over 40 years ago. He wrote that, self-efficacy is "the conviction that one can success-fully execute the behavior required to produce outcomes" (p. 193). In other words, it is the belief that you are capable of successfully performing activities that produce a specific result. Bandura (1997) indicated that, "self-efficacy is concerned not with the number of skills you have, but with what you believe you can do with what you have under a variety of circumstances" (p. 37). Self-efficacy beliefs are a principal contributor to how well one performs, no matter the domain and skills needed (Bandura, 1992).

Bandura's self-efficacy theory influenced the development of the concepts of teacher self-efficacy and collective teacher efficacy. Donohoo (2017) noted that, "Teacher self-efficacy refers to a teacher's belief that he or she can perform the necessary activities to influence learning" (p. 43). It is important to understand that teacher self-efficacy is about a teacher's perception of their abilities rather than an unbiased evaluation of the teacher's competence. Related to teacher self-efficacy is collective teacher efficacy. Tschannen-Moran and Barr (2004) described collective teacher efficacy as the "collective self-perception that teachers in a given school make an educational difference to their students over and above the educational impact of their homes and communities" (p. 190). According to Donohoo (2017), "Collective efficacy is high when teachers believe that the staff is capable of helping students master complex content, fostering students' creativity, and getting students to believe they can do well in school" (p. 3). Hattie and Zierer (2018) add that, "Teachers' collective efficacy refers to the enhanced confidence to overcome any barriers and limitations and have the collective belief that all students in this school can gain more than a year's growth for a year's input" (p. 26).

Hattie and Zierer (2018) indicated, in *10 Mindframes for Visible Learning: Teaching for Success*, that collective teacher efficacy is the greatest factor in influencing student success. This statement was based on Hattie's meta-analysis research studies where he examined and ranked 138 (Hattie, 2009) and 195 (Hattie, 2012) factors influencing student achievement. Hattie discovered that collective teacher efficacy outranked all other factors including socioeconomic status, parental involvement, home environment, and prior achievement. We change agents—especially collectively—play a critical role in the success of our learners.

It is crucial as change agents to understand the power we can have on the success of our learners. Our actions can and do have direct consequences on the progress our learners make. We must believe that we have the ability to bring about positive changes in our classrooms and schools. As Bandura (1997) wrote, "Unless people believe they can produce desired effects by their actions, they have little incentive to act" (p. 2). So, as change agents, not only is it important to believe in our own abilities, it is also important to help the educators we work with understand the impact teacher self-efficacy and collective teacher efficacy can have on learner achievement.

Research to Consider: Educator Self-Efficacy, Self-Directed Professional Development, and Voxer

For an interesting read about the impact self-directed professional development can have on educator self-efficacy, we suggest reading a chapter by Jeff Carpenter and Tim Green. The chapter focuses on how educators used Voxer as a tool to facilitate their own professional development.

Carpenter, J., & Green, T. (2018). Self-directed professional learning and educator self-efficacy: The case of Voxer. In C. B. Hodges (Ed.), *Self-efficacy in instructional technology contexts* (pp. 163–181). New York, NY: Springer.

Sources of Self-Efficacy

So, how might we go about helping learners and educators (and ourselves) enhance self-efficacy beliefs? Bandura (1997) indicated that our beliefs about our self-efficacy are developed from four primary sources of information. The information serves as feedback that changes how we perceive our abilities. These sources of information are as follows:

- mastery experiences,
- vicarious experiences,
- verbal persuasion, and
- physiological and affective states.

Mastery experiences are the most "influential source of efficacy information because they provide the most authentic evidence of whether one can muster whatever it takes to succeed" (Bandura, 1997, p. 80). These types of experiences allow learners to demonstrate their competence or mastery in a given situation. The more success a learner has in situations, the greater a learner's perception of his or her abilities will be. This success helps a learner build their self-efficacy. It is important to know that Bandura (1997) indicates that failure can weaken self-efficacy; specifically if the failure occurs prior to a learner's self-efficacy being largely established. This is an important point considering the current notion in PK-12 education that learners should be allowed to fail and embrace it. Bandura (1986) indicates that once an individual has a strong sense of self-efficacy, infrequent failures will be unlikely to significantly affect an individual's self-efficacy.

Vicarious experience is based on modeling. Bandura (1997) suggested "seeing or visualizing people similar to oneself perform successfully typically raises efficacy beliefs in observers that they themselves possess the capabilities to master comparable activities" (p. 87). So, if learners see others who they believe are like themselves doing something successfully, then the learners are likely to believe they have the same capability. Think of this in light of what we discussed about Opinion Leaders in Part I, Chapter 4.

Verbal persuasion focuses on others persuading learners to believe that they have the capabilities needed to succeed. Bandura (1997) indicated that, "People who are persuaded verbally that they possess the capabilities to master given tasks are likely to mobilize greater effort and sustain it than if they harbor self-doubts and dwell on personal deficiencies when difficulties arise" (p. 101). However, simply convincing learners that they can be successful is not sufficient enough in helping them succeed. The conditions necessary to perform effectively must be provided. Without these conditions, the likely outcome will be failure along with the mistrust of the persuader. Bandura (1997) indicate that this situation could undermine the learner's perceived self-efficacy (p. 198). We are sure you made the connection between this and your role as a change agent in supporting others during the change process and innovation adoption.

Physiological and affective states can have an impact on self-efficacy beliefs. Learners cognitively process information affecting the body (i.e., somatic information) that is delivered by physiological and emotional states. Learners take this information and make judgements about how the information influences their performance. Learners often "read their somatic arousal in stressful or taxing situations as ominous signs of vulnerability to dysfunction" (Bandura, 1997, p. 107). There are ways to improve self-efficacy beliefs by working on neutralizing how learners react to physiological and affective states. Helping learners "to enhance physical status, reduce stress levels and negative emotional proclivities, and correct misinterpretations of bodily states" (p. 107) can help improve self-efficacy beliefs if they are associated with improvements in an individual's performance (Bandura, 1986).

Understanding what influences the development of self-efficacy can help you as a change agent. As you facilitate the change process and innovation adoption, it is important to understand that self-efficacy beliefs have tremendous influence on how individuals react and what they do. Donohoo (2017) indicated that, "Efficacy beliefs are very powerful because they guide educators' action and behavior. Efficacy beliefs help determine what educators focus on, how they respond to challenges, and how they expend their efforts" (p. xv). White (1982) indicated that, "a resilient sense of efficacy enables individuals to do extraordinary things by productive use of their skills in the face of overwhelming obstacles" (p. 37). This is exactly the mindset we want those to have who we are asking to change and adopt innovations. According to Bandura (1997), however, "If people believe they have no power to produce results, they will not attempt to make things happen" (p. 3).

 ## Research to Consider: Hattie's Visible Learning Research

We mentioned John Hattie's (2009, 2012) research that examined and ranked factors influencing student achievement. The research method used for these studies was meta-analysis. Although it is beyond the scope of this book to describe the intricacies of meta-analysis research, we believe it is important for you to understand a few basics. This method is based on a statistical analysis that combines results from multiple studies to determine an effect size. The effect size, according to Richard Coe (2002), "is particularly valuable for quantifying the effectiveness of a particular intervention, relative to some comparison. It allows us to move beyond the simplistic, 'Does it work or not?' to the far more sophisticated, 'How well does it work in a range of contexts?'" (para. 2). With Hattie's research, he focused on studies that dealt with student achievement. He was interested in discovering what factors (e.g., class size, teacher-student relationships) had the greatest influence on improving student achievement. These were categorized into six domains: curriculum, family, learners, school, teacher, and teaching (Hattie & Zierer, 2018). Despite our admiration for this work, it is important to understand that there is criticism of it (Hattie and Zierer admit to it having flaws). We highly suggest that you read the work by Barrie Bennett about effect size to understand some of the criticism about meta-analysis research and the approach Hattie used. We have provided a reference to Bennett's work along with three other resources in case you want to explore.

Bennett, B. (2018). Critique: What effect size doesn't tell us. In G. E. Hall, L. F. Quinn, & D. M. Gollnick (Eds.), *The Wiley handbook of teaching and learning* (pp. 431–444). Hoboken, NJ: Wiley Blackwell.

Coe, R. (2002). *It's the effect size, stupid: What effect size is and why it is important.* Paper presented at the Annual Conference of the British Educational Research Association, University of Exeter, England. Retrieved from https://www.leeds.ac.uk/educol/documents/00002182.htm

Hattie, J. (2009). *Visible learning.* London, England: Routledge.

Hattie, J. (2012). *Visible learning for teachers.* London, England: Routledge.

The iMakers

There is no denying that the world our PK-12 learners live in is different in many ways from the one we experienced when we were in PK-12. Our learners have grown up immersed in a digital world where they are surrounded by computer-based technology with 24-hour, 7 days a week access to a seemingly endless amount of information and people from around the world. As such, our learners view their world and interact with it almost exclusively through a technology lens. Most everything they do throughout their day involves the use of some form of computer-based technology. Our learners live and breathe technology in all that they do.

Helping our learners become effective users of technology for learning requires that we have a clear understanding of exactly who they are. This understanding includes knowing how they view the world, how they learn, and how they picture being ideally engaged in learning in and out of school. Additionally, helping our learners become effective users of technology for learning also requires that we have a complete understanding of the skills they need to be contemporary learners.

This chapter focuses on both of these areas—describing who our learners are and identifying the skills they need to become successful learners who have the knowledge and skills necessary to compete in a global economy. Although the chapter has distinct sections, they help provide you with a comprehensive understanding of your learners when considered collectively. We begin the chapter with a profile of a typical learner we have in our classrooms—who we refer to as an iMaker. We discuss how we developed the iMaker profile. We then move into a discussion of how the iMakers prefer to engage in learning. Again, the goal of this chapter is to help you better understand the learners you serve. We believe that the more you know about your learners, the more effective you can be in creating a teaching and learning environment that uses educational technology to help them reach their potential and become successful contemporary learners.

Our Profile of PK-12 Learners

There has been no shortage of terms since 2000 to describe generations of PK-12 students who have grown up in a time where networked digital technology has been ubiquitous. Several popular press books (e.g., Oblinger & Oblinger, 2005; Prensky, 2001; Rosen, Carrier, & Cheever, 2010; Seemiller & Grace, 2019; Strauss & Howe, 2001; Tapscott, 1999, 2009; Twenge, 2018) have provided descriptions of these generations of students—the Net Generation, Generation Next, digital natives, Generation M, Millennials, the iGeneration, Gen Y, and Gen Z. Several of these books have been provocative. They have started conversations about how those growing up in a networked world have taken advantage of and have been influenced by networked digital-technology. Although these books have helped educators consider how we educate PK-12 learners, we believe we are at a time when PK-12 education needs to push the conversation forward and reconsider teaching and learning.

 Point to Consider: Avoiding the Dichotomy of Digital Natives and Digital Immigrants

There is no doubt that you have read or heard the terms digital native and digital immigrant. These terms describe the notion that PK-12 learners ("digital natives") have innate abilities for using technology that adults ("digital immigrants") do not have. This often-repeated myth has been in the literature for the past two decades. It is an unfortunate and unnecessary dichotomy that we continue to read about and hear. It is one that we wish would disappear. Although there is little argument that PK-12 learners often are more willing

---

than adults to take risks with using technology, there is no objective evidence that PK-12 learners are better at using technology. This is especially true when it comes to using technology for learning (Koutropoulos, 2011). Numerous researchers (e.g., Brown & Czerniewicz, 2010; Facer & Furlong 2001; Helsper & Eynon, 2010; Kennedy, Judd, Dalgarnot, & Waycott, 2010; Margarayn, Littlejohn, & Vojt, 2011) have critiqued the narrow labeling of learners based solely on their exposure to technology. Brown and Czerniewicz indicated that the notion of the digital native is an "othering" concept and that it sets up a "binary opposition" between the alleged digital natives and digital immigrants (p. 1). They went on to state that, "This polarization makes the concept less flexible and more determinist in that it implies that if a person falls into one category, they cannot exhibit characteristics of the other category" (p. 1). Bennett and Maton (2010) added, "While this body of work provides a preliminary understanding, it also highlights subtleties and complexities that require further investigation. It suggests, for example, that we must go beyond simple dichotomies evident in the digital native debate to develop a more sophisticated understanding of our students' experiences of technology" (p. 321). So, the next time you hear these terms or you want to repeat them, please pause and consider whether the terms are helpful in describing learners and change agents.

We developed the iMaker profile (Green & Donovan, 2018) to better understand our learners. The iMaker profile is not meant to create a dichotomy between PK-12 learners and those who are involved in educating them. The profile is also not meant to provide a narrow description that imposes a strict set of characteristics, dispositions, and desires on our learners. Rather, the goal is to provide an updated view on PK-12 learners that leads to conversations on how to approach and to best serve the needs of the learners we have in our classrooms and will have for the foreseeable future.

We developed the iMaker profile through our work with educators and learners in schools. In developing our profile, we have drawn from a number of sources including our own research (e.g., Donovan, Green, & Hartley, 2010; Donovan, Green, & Mason, 2014). Specifically, the profile is influenced by the work of Don Tapscott (2009) regarding the Net Generation and Generation Next, Rosen et al.'s (2010) discussion of the iGeneration, and the research of Lee Martin (2015) on the maker movement in education. The profile is a composite of salient attributes from these various perspectives. Despite these resources being 5–10 years old, as of the writing of this book, we believe they provide significant insights into understanding our learners.

We used the term iMakers because we believe this acknowledges their interconnectedness with networked digital technologies and their engagement in aspects associated with the maker culture. Although our profile is not a major departure from other descriptions of PK-12 learners, it is an extension and provides for a revised view of P-12 students. We know that there will be disagreement with what we describe. We encourage disagreement that is civil. It can be healthy and productive if it helps us better understand our learners. So, as you read the profile, keep in mind our primary goal of providing a comprehensive perspective of our current PK-12 students that can lead to productive conversations about how to best meet their learning needs.

 Point to Consider: Generations X, Y, and Z

Individuals have been labeled and described as generations since the beginning of the 20th century in the United States. Strauss and Howe (2000) defined a social generation as the collection of people born over a span of approximately 20 years. According to Strauss and Howe, a generation shares three criteria: (1) they encounter key historical and social events during the same phase of life, (2) they share common beliefs and behaviors that were shaped based on the era when they were children and young adults, and (3) they are aware of the experiences and traits they share with their peers, which leads to a perceived membership of a generation. There have been six generations since 1900: the Greatest Generation (1900–1924), the Silent Generation (1925–1945), the Baby Boomers (1946–1964), Generation X (1965–1979), Generation Y or millennials (1980–late

1990s), and the current generation, Gen Z or iGen (late 1990s to 2010s) (Dimock, 2019). Although defining individuals as generations can be limiting, it can help us better understand their lived experiences and how their beliefs and behaviors were shaped. It can provide us with a basis to discuss their needs. This is why we coined the term the iMaker Generation (in 2016) to describe learners who are currently in PK-12. Although most were born in the 2000s, we believe that the characteristics of the iMakers we describe in this chapter fit learners who are also finishing high school and many learners who are currently undergraduates in college, and it describes those who will be attending school in the years to come. We hesitated to provide an exact age range because this suggests an evanescent nature of our iMaker profile, which we believe is not accurate (however, only time will tell).

Three Additional Perspectives of PK-12 Learners

Before we describe the iMaker profile, let's review the three perspectives we mentioned that influenced the profile in case you are not familiar with them or if it has been awhile since you last read about them. Table 8.1 outlines the salient elements of the three perspectives. Tapscott indicated that the Net Generation as being from 1977 through 1997 and the Generation Next beginning in 1998 and through 2008, which was when he finished writing his book, *Grown Up Digital*. In this book, Tapscott (2009) outlined "8 differentiating characteristics of the Net Generation Norms" (p. 34). He described that each norm is a grouping of behaviors and attitudes that help define the Net Generation and Generation Next. These help us understand how the generation views learning, work, the family, markets, and society. Rosen, et al. (2010) created the term *iGeneration* to describe preschool, elementary, and secondary school–aged children born in the 1990s and the start of the new millennium. They identified nine characteristics that this generation shares. Martin (2015) wrote about the beliefs and dispositions that make up the Maker Mindset. This mindset helps individuals actively engage in a maker environment and in the maker community (p. 35).

Table 8.1 Salient Elements of the Three Perspectives

Generation Next (Tapscott, 2009)	iGeneration (Rosen et al., 2010)	The Maker Mindset (Martin, 2015)
They express themselves freely over different mediums and want to make choices without being limited by rules and regulations.	They are motivation-driven and seek positive reinforcement. They want to be told they are doing good work and have constant reinforcement as they are working.	Those who have a maker mindset are interested in engaging in activities that are playful and fun. They find these activities to be intrinsically motivating. Martin described the work of Hatano and Inagaki (1986) that suggested a playful learning environment encourages experimentation and the experience of variation. These two elements can help develop conceptual knowledge and adaptive expertise (p. 35).
They adapt, modify, and personalize every aspect of their lives from the content they consume to their work environments.	They are family-oriented and enjoy spending time with their family. Many live at their parent's home and want them involved in their educational experiences.	Those with a maker mindset build on their areas of strength and develop skills and learn new information, as needed, as they engage in activities that interest them. They are not afraid to make mistakes and engage in situations that are new and possibly uncomfortable. Martin describes this disposition as being consistent with the concept of growth-mindset where failure is "interpreted as an indicator that more effort is required, rather than a cue to disengage" (p. 35).
They want access to relevant news and information to analyze and critique companies and their products, the government, and other organizations.	They are extremely confident about their abilities. Rosen et al. stated that they "exude a confident air that surpasses that of any prior generation" (p. 47).	Those who have a maker mindset are not afraid to make mistakes and fail. They do not look at failure with disdain, but rather as part of a process of improving a product. Chic (2011) indicated that the process of overcoming obstacles ultimately leads makers to have a better understanding of how to address future problems and develop expertise.

Their values need to be matched in all that they do—especially with companies they work for and those they are a consumer

They want some element of play and entertainment in all aspects of their lives.

They prefer to collaborate and build a wide range of relationships.

They want to access data and communicate in real time.

They desire to continuously innovate and change the way they learn, work, and communicate.

They are more open to change than earlier generations (Lyons, Duxbury, & Higgins, 2007). Rosen et al. indicated that they value change "as evidenced by how they flock to any new innovation at lightning speed. Remember, this is the generation that Play" (p. 68).

They want to connect with their peers and others (throughout the world) in and out of the classroom to collaborate and engage in conversations. They enjoy the social aspects of learning.

They have a need to respond to others and to access information immediately.

Those with a maker mindset enjoy sharing and collaborating (although they do work alone as well). Typically, they freely share their knowledge and are willing to help others. This can lead to the development of collective knowledge and what Zhang et al. (2012) have described as knowledge building communities.

The iMaker Profile Defined

We recognize that every learner is unique. Each brings to the classroom a distinct set of abilities, experiences, needs, and preferences that affect how the learner approaches learning. As such, we cannot treat all learners exactly the same. Despite their uniqueness, we believe, as others do, that there are general statements that can be made about our learners. These statements provide us with an overview or perspective of our learners that we can use to help design learning environments that effectively meet their needs. This is why we developed our iMaker profile.

The iMaker profile was developed to help educators think deeply and deliberately about the learners in schools. As we mentioned, it is important to consider learners beyond their abilities and physical characteristics if we are to create learning environments that meet their needs. You will notice, as you read the iMaker profile, that the iMakers share elements across the three perspectives described in Table 8.1. Despite sharing these elements, the iMaker profile is specifically unique.

The iMakers' characteristics focus on the concept of *making*—learning that takes place as a result of creating something that is shared publicly (Papert & Harel, 1991). These characteristics are as follows:

- **Making Their Learning Environments.** iMakers have a distinct desire to have control of their learning. They want their learning to be meaningful and relevant to their lives. They want a personalized learning environment that they have been directly involved in creating.

- **Making Play and Experimentation Part of Learning.** No matter what the learning environment or context is, iMakers want it to include elements of play and experimentation. Many iMakers are gamers who want and enjoy learning that includes game-like elements that make learning feel like play. iMakers want the opportunity to experiment with new ideas and technologies before they adopt them into their lives.

- **Making Through DIY and DIWO.** iMakers have a do-it-yourself (DIY) and do-it-with-others (DIWO) mentality. They want opportunities to create without being prescribed how they go about the process and what the final product or outcome should be. They want to have these opportunities to learn on their own and with others.

- **Making Learning Anywhere, Anytime.** iMakers do not view school as the only place where learning takes place. With their abundant access to networked technologies, they have access to data and can communicate in real time. iMakers learn in a variety of contexts with and from a wide range of individuals—not only their teachers and classmates. iMakers do not want to be limited to when, how, and with whom learning occurs.

- **Making Through Remixing and Mash-Ups.** iMakers have a remix and mash-up orientation when it comes to creating ideas and products. They view themselves as content creators rather than just consumers of content. iMakers want to be able to use ideas, concepts, and products from others—along with their own—to create something new, different, or unique.

- **Making Sense of Change and Innovation.** iMakers are not opposed to change and innovation. They are able to adapt and modify different aspects of their lives as needed. They are quick to try new technologies and embrace them if they are able to modify the technologies to fit their specific needs.

- **Making Their Voices Heard.** iMakers want their voices to be heard. They have the desire to share with a wide audience the ideas and products they make. They do so for different reasons—to receive feedback, to learn new skills and ideas, and to engage in reflection.

- **Making Connections to Communities.** iMakers have a strong desire to belong to a community. Often, they are members of multiple and diverse virtual and face-to-face communities. They are capable of being active and engaged in these multiple communities simultaneously. Based on their personal needs, iMakers often jump in and out of communities (Green & Donovan, 2018).

 # Point to Consider: The Maker Movement in Education

The maker movement has had a direct influence on PK-12 education. Halverson and Sheridan (2014) describe that the maker movement "refers broadly to the growing number of people who are engaged in the creative production of artifacts in their daily lives and who find physical and digital forums to share their processes and products with others" (p. 496). The movement has been embraced in part because it fits with the increased emphasis on STEM education. We see the emergence of makerspaces in PK-12 schools as result of this embrace. It is important to consider the elements of an effective maker learning environment. It goes beyond just a makerspace. According to Martin (2014), there are three necessary elements: digital tools, a community infrastructure, and the maker mindset. Digital tools are the technologies (e.g., 3D printers, mobile devices) that allow individuals to design and make products. The community infrastructure includes the community of individuals that "has arisen around making" along with "the infrastructure that supports community engagement" (p. 34) in the making process. The maker mindset is the combination of values and dispositions that "typify participation in the community" (Martin, 2014, p. 35). Halverson and Sheridan (2014) discussed three similar elements that define the maker movement. These are "... *making* as a set of activities, *makerspaces* as communities of practice, and *makers* as identities ..." (p. 496). Hatch (2014) characterized the maker movement has having nine elements: make, share, give, learn, tool up, play, participate, support, and change. Again, it is important to keep in mind that it involves more than just designing and create products—in other words, it is more than just a makerspace in a corner of the classroom. Sharples et al. (2013) wrote that it "encompasses not only the process of creating specific objects, but also the social and learning cultures surrounding their construction" (p. 33).

Digital Technology

A teaching and learning environment that meets the needs of all learners requires that learners and educators have access to a variety of technology. Access to technology provides unique opportunities for learners to develop skills needed to be true contemporary learners. Access alone, however, will not ensure that these opportunities are effective (Green & Donovan, 2018). Effective learning opportunities are created by educators who have a solid understanding of the types of educational technology available *and* what technologies are designed to do. Helping you gain this type of understanding is the primary goal of this chapter. In helping meet this goal, we outline and describe an approach we developed to help educators make sense of the vast amount of technology available and to thoughtfully consider the technology they use in their teaching. Our approach includes several elements that we will share—technology integration models, important terms, a framework for considering technology use, and keeping current with trends and issues. By the end of the chapter, you will be in a solid position to facilitate change that involves the adoption of digital technology.

Talking the Talk of Educational Technology

There are numerous terms and jargon associated with technology and the use of technology in PK-12 education that are important for you to know as a change agent. Knowing these terms and what they represent will help you better communicate with those you are working with as you facilitate the change process. It can be extremely difficult to facilitate change and

Point to Consider: Contemporary Rather than 21st-Century

Although the terms 21st-century learning, 21st-century skills, 21st-century teaching, and 21st-century technology are entrenched in the vernacular of education, we believe it is time for a change. We prefer to replace 21st century with *contemporary* to signify that what is being referred to is current. Despite this being a term we do take credit for developing, it is difficult to determine who coined this term. The earliest mention of this term that we can locate is from the Australian Ministerial Council on Education, Employment, Training, and Youth Affairs (MCEETYA) report in 2005 titled "Contemporary Learning: Learning in an Online World." The report discussed the approach to learning for students in Australia and New Zealand. So, consider replacing 21st century with contemporary when you use these terms. Let's see if we can get this to catch on. We use the term contemporary throughout the book.

the adoption of a technology-based innovation if you and those you are working with have different definitions and understandings of these terms.

We include 12 common terms that we use and come across frequently. The terms are listed alphabetically. You will notice that a term may include another term in its description (e.g., *apps* include the term *device*). The descriptions are based on our understanding of the professional literature and how we use the terms. As you read through the remaining sections of this chapter and come across these terms, having read through these definitions will provide you with a clearer understanding of what is being discussed.

21st-Century Skills. This term was made prominent by the Partnership for 21st-Century Skills (P21), which is now part of the Battelle for Kids network (http://www.battelleforkids.org/networks/p21). The Partnership for 21st-Century Skills was formed in 2002 through a collaborative effort of the U.S. Department of Education and a variety of private organizations (AOL Time Warner Foundation; Apple Computer, Inc.; Cable in the Classroom; Cisco Systems, Inc.; Dell Computer Corporation; Microsoft Corporation; National Education Association; SAP). The Partnership created a framework

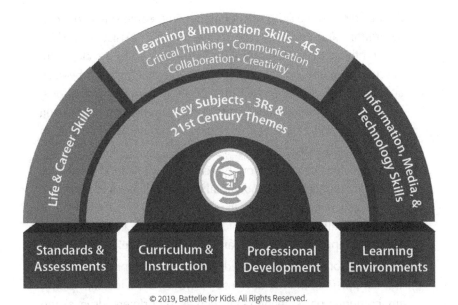

Figure 9.1 Framework for 21st century learning, Reproduced by permission of Battelle for Kids (2019)

(see Figure 9.1) to "define and illustrate the skills and knowledge students need to succeed in work and life, as well as the support systems necessary for 21st-Century learning outcomes" (Battelle for Kids, 2019, para. 1). Part of this framework included what they defined as the 4 Cs: critical thinking, communication, collaboration, and creativity. Although you will find the term *21st-century skills* used quite frequently, we prefer to use the term *contemporary skills* (see Point to Consider: Contemporary Rather than 21st Century). We believe it is time to update this term because we are well into the 21st century. You will also find similar terms used—*21st-century technology*, *21st-century teaching*, and *21st-century learning*. We believe that these terms should be updated as well.

21st-Century Learning and 21st-Century Teaching. These terms refer to teaching and learning that focus on helping learners gain the contemporary skills and knowledge needed to be successful in a globally connected and digitally networked world. Twenty-first-century teaching and learning is often associated with the use of technology, educators as facilitators, learners engaged in inquiry and problem-solving, and active pedagogy and assessment.

4 Cs. This refers to the skills of critical thinking, communication, collaboration, and creativity. The Partnership for 21st-Century Skills created this term to describe skills learners need to be successful in school and beyond. It is important to note that there has been an update—the *7 Cs* (Trilling & Fadel, 2009) that includes additional skills of cross-cultural understanding, communication, computing technology, and career learning. You will come across this term less frequently than the 4 Cs.

Apps. App is short for application. Typically, an application is software that is downloaded by an individual to a mobile device. However, an app can refer to software that is downloaded on any type of hardware platform (e.g., Android®, iOS®, OS®, or Windows®). We often hear app used to refer to any type of software.

Device. Most often, device is used to refer to smartphones, tablets, and laptops (i.e., mobile devices). However, a device can refer to any computer-based technology such as 3D printers, drones, and robots.

Digital Technology. Digital technology refers to computer-based products and solutions. It is used as a generic term that refers to any computer-based device. This is typically what we are referring to when using this term and when we use the term *technology*.

Educational Technology. Januszewski and Molenda (2008) describe educational technology as "the study and ethical practice of facilitating learning and improving performance by creating, using, and managing appropriate technological processes and resources" (p. 1). The key elements from this definition are the focus on facilitating learning and improving performance through technology and the processes that technology affords. Educational technology, therefore, is more than just the devices and apps that we use. Often, though, when this term is used, what is being described are devices and apps.

Emerging Technology. An emerging technology is one that is new or one that is developing or evolving. Often, this refers to technology that is not widely available but that most likely will be in 3–5 years.

Instructional Technology. Instructional Technology is defined by Seels and Richey (2012) as "the theory and practice of design, development, utilization, management, and evaluation of processes and resources for learning" (p. 1). Although you may find instructional technology and educational technology used synonymously, they have different meanings and intentions. Educational technology focuses on the use of technology while instructional technology focuses more on technology. It is important to understand that there is a difference, and that this viewpoint is not shared by all.

Student-Centered Use of Technology. This refers to the use of technology by learners in ways that they give them the control over the where, when, and how technology is used.

Technology. The term technology refers to the practical application of knowledge to solve problems or invent useful tools. Typically, though, the term is used as a generic umbrella term to describe any computer-based technology. Technology is often used synonymously with digital technology or computer-based technology. When we use the term technology in this book, we are referring to computer-based technology (e.g., laptops, smartphones, 3D printers).

Technology-Rich Learning Environment/Technology-Rich Classroom. This refers to learning environments where learners and educators have access to a variety of technology. These learning environments are networked and connected to the Internet.

Tools. This is a generic term referring to any digital technology (e.g., device or app) that is being used by learners or educators. We use the term tool to indicate that technology is one part of the teaching and learning process that when used with effective pedagogy can assist learners in gaining contemporary skills and knowledge. In other words, technology is simply one of many tools educators (and learners) have to help improve learning.

PK-12 Learner Access to Technology

We discussed in Chapter 8 (The iMakers) that our learners have grown up surrounded by networked computer-based technology that has afforded them with seemingly limitless and immediate access to information and people from around the world. Their view of and interactions with their world is through this lens of technology. As we consider this, it is important to have a clear understanding of the technology our learners have access to outside of the classroom. Although there is research and resources (e.g., Brown & Green, 2018, 2019; Delgado, Wardlow, McKnight, & O'Malley, 2005; National Science Board, 2018; Project Tomorrow, 2019) that describe learners' access to educational technology in schools, we focus on the technology learners have outside of school because this keeps the emphasis on our learners who are the focus of this chapter and it also places the emphasis on learning anytime, anywhere through technology (see Chapter 10).

Our goal with this section PK-12 learner access to technology is to provide you with a general overview. We have found that a holistic perspective can help change agents as we make decisions during the change process and innovation adoption. Rather than making assumptions about technology access our learners have, we need to start with a foundation of information that informs and guides our actions.

A Look-Back and a Recent Look

We start with a look-back to 2010 with a published report from the Kaiser Family Foundation—*Generation M2: Media in the Lives of 8- to 18-Year-Olds*. This report, at that time, was one of the most comprehensive survey research reports available on the access to and use of media by American youth. The Kaiser Family Foundation sponsored the research that was carried out three times—1999, 2004, and 2009. Participants in the latest report included a sample of more than 2,000 young people throughout the United States. Those surveyed were from a wide-range of socioeconomic, race, and age groups. The report indicated that young people had ever-increasing access to technology and media. According to the report, the typical 8- to 18-year-old's home contained on average the following devices (yes, some of this technology might be considered relics now, but keep in mind that the data is from 2009):

- 3.8 TVs
- 2.8 DVD or VCR players
- 2.5 radios

- 2.3 console video-game players
- 2.2 CD players
- 2 computers
- 1 digital video recorder

The data showed a steady increase in access from 1999 to 2009 of all devices, except for radios and CD players. In looking at the data more narrowly, 99% of the youth indicated having at least one TV in their home, and 71% indicated having a TV in their room. Ninety-three percent indicated having at least one computer at home and 36% indicated having a computer in their bedroom. The most significant increase in access to technology was with mobile devices. When considering all 8- to 18-year-olds surveyed for the Kaiser report in 2009, 76% indicated owning an iPod®/MP3 player (18% in 2004), 66% owned a cell phone (39% in 2004), and 29% owned a laptop (12% in 2004). In addition to an increase in access to mobile devices, there was an increase in home access to the Internet, with 84% reporting having access. Of this percentage, 59% indicated that they had high-speed or wireless access, and 33% indicated having Internet access in their bedroom (Rideout, Foehr, & Roberts, 2010). There were significant increases to technology access in the 5-year period from 2004 to 2009.

Project Tomorrow's annual *Speak Up* report from 2010 corroborated many of the findings in the Kaiser report. The 2010 *Speak Up* report addressed personal access and use of technology of U.S. K-12 students, focusing specifically on mobile devices and online learning. This annual report included responses from 294,399 K-12 students throughout the United States (Project Tomorrow, 2011). The report focused on mobile technology. The data indicated that the highest level of access to mobile technology across grade levels was MP3 players and laptops. Eighty-five percent of high school students had access to an MP3 player, while 37% of K-2 students had access. Access to laptops for high school students was 67 and 37% for K-2 students. Student cell phone access (without Internet access) ranged from 21% for K-2 students to 56% for high school students. Access to smartphones was slightly lower, with a range of 16% for K-2 students to 44% for high school students. Student access to a tablet device for all grade levels was a low of 8% for students in grades 3–5 and a high of 13% for students in grades 6–8.

Two recent reports—*Teens, Social Media and Technology* and the *Speak Up Research Initiative, 2017–2018 Findings*—provide insight into the current levels of personal access our learners have. The Pew Research Center report, *Teens, Social Media and Technology*, indicated that 95% of teens (ages 13–17) surveyed (n = 743, randomly sampled throughout the United States) indicated that they have or have access to a smartphone. This is up to 22% from teens surveyed in 2014–2015 for a similar report. According to the 2018 report, "Smartphone ownership is nearly universal among teens of different genders, races and ethnicities and socioeconomic backgrounds" (Anderson & Jiang, 2018, p. 7). However, this is not the same for access to a home computer. Despite 88% indicating having access to a home computer, the access varied significantly by income level. Ninety-six percent of teens from households reporting an annual income of $75,000 or more reported having access, while 75% of teens from households earning less than $30,000 a year reported having access. Access varied by parent education level. Ninety-four percent of teens who have a parent with an undergraduate degree were more likely to indicate having access to a home computer as compared to 78% of teens whose parents have a high school diploma or less (Anderson & Jiang, 2018, p. 8). The *Speak Up Research Initiative, 2017–18 Findings* (Project Tomorrow, 2018b) reported similar personal access levels for students surveyed (340,927 K-12 students). Table 9.1 shows the personal access K-12 students have to various mobile devices. According to data from the latest *Speak Up* report from 2018, "81% of middle school students and 92% of high school students having personal access to a smartphone" (Evans, 2019, p. 6)—a slight increase from the previous report.

Table 9.1 Personal Access K-12 Students

Students	Smartphone (%)	Tablet (%)	Laptop (%)	Digital Reader (%)	Smartwatch (%)
Grade 9–12	91	39	54	13	12
Grade 6–8	79	55	48	14	15
Grade 3–5	50	57	35	15	
Grade K-2	35	53	32	10	

There are several important ideas that we believe emerge from the data. The primary one we observed is that our learners indeed have personal access to technology, and the level of access continues to increase. The second important idea is that access levels to some devices are relatively high—specifically smartphones and especially for our learners who are teens. The third idea, and a very important one to understand, is that student access to technology is not reserved only for students from a particular school-community type, ethnicity, economic level, or gender. Students of all types have ever-increasing personal access to technology.

 Point to Consider: Learners' Use of Technology Outside of School

We've shared the personal access level learners have had and have to technology outside of school. Let's take a brief look at how our learners have used and are using technology outside of school. *Generation M2: Media in the Lives of 8- to 18-Year-Olds* indicated that 8- to 18 year-olds spent an average of 7 hours and 38 minutes using entertainment media throughout a typical day. This is an increase of an hour and 18 minutes for this age group when comparing it to data from 2005 (Rideout et al., 2010). During these 7.5 hours, multiple forms of media were being used at one time—this translates into 10 hours and 45 minutes of media content being packed into the 7.5 hours (Rideout et al., 2010, 2). The 2018 report from the Pew Research Center (*Teens, Social Media and Technology*) indicated that 45% of teens say they are online on a near-constant basis and 44% indicated being online multiple times a day (Anderson & Jiang, 2018). This is 89% of our teen learners being online at least multiple times a day. These reports clearly indicate that our learners are using technology outside of school. As change agents, we need to consider how we can take advantage of this to engage them in learning outside the classroom. We highly suggest that you take a look at both reports to get a more in-depth understanding of the data.

Technology Integration Models

A technology integration model provides a framework for how to approach the use of technology to enhance learning. It is important for change agents to have an understanding of what a technology integration model is because it can be a useful tool. There are several exceptionally popular models that you will regularly encounter. We provide a caution, however, about technology integration models—they are often misused. They should be used to provide guidance on how to consider and reflect on technology use for teaching and learning rather than as a prescription for how and when technology is used. The how and when of technology use are decisions that are best left to change agents who understand their learners and the complexities of the teaching and learning environment where the technology will be integrated. Additionally, it is important to note that some technology integration models have research support but many do not. We do not want to leave the impression that technology integration models are not useful. On the contrary, they can be highly useful if the intent is known and they are used for that intent.

Several technology integration models have been developed since 2000 that have had an impact on how technology is considered and used in PK-12 education. We discuss four models that are popular— the Partnership for 21st Century Learning Framework (2002), Mishra and Koehler's (2006) TPACK (Technological, Pedagogical, and Content Knowledge) Framework, Ruben Puentedura's (2006) SAMR (Substitution, Augmentation, Modification, Redefinition) Model, and the Technology Integration Matrix (TIM) (2007). Again, these models provide guidance on how to consider the meaningful integration of technology. We provide a general overview of each model. We encourage you to read more about these models in the "Digging Deeper" section at the end of Part II.

The Partnership for 21st-Century Learning Framework

As mentioned earlier in the chapter, the Partnership for 21st-century learning (P21; now part of the Battelle Network for Kids) developed their initial P21 Framework in 2007. The initial framework for 21st-century skills was a graphic of a rainbow arch that highlighted 21st-century student outcomes and support systems (see Figure 9.1). The outcomes focused on learning content—the three "Rs" and 21st-century themes related to history, science, and world languages—as well as life and career skills, information and communication technology (ICT) and media skills, and learning and innovations skills, and the 4Cs. The development of the 4 Cs—critical thinking, communication, collaboration, and creativity—was the primary focus. The initial framework has since been updated from focusing primarily on skills to focusing on what they refer to as 21st-century teaching and learning. The Partnership for 21st-century learning has been tremendously influential in shaping how educators view the contemporary skills needed to be successful in a globally connected and digitally networked world.

The TPACK Framework

The various elements of the Technological Pedagogical and Content Knowledge Framework (TPACK) are depicted in Figure 9.2. Matthew

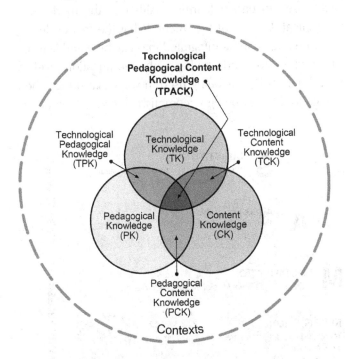

Figure 9.2 The Technological Pedagogical Content Knowledge (TPACK) framework. Reproduced by permission of the publisher (tpack.org, 2012)

Koehler and Punya Mishra (2009), the developers of TPACK, describe it as a "framework for teacher knowledge for technology integration" (p. 60). The primary outcome of the framework is to help educators become highly effective practitioners by being proficient in all areas—technology, pedagogy, and content knowledge. Koehler and Mishra indicate that integrating technology in an effective manner requires educators to have more than just skill in using technology. Educators must also be skilled in pedagogy and experienced in the content being taught. It is the mixture of these three areas that fosters the most effective integration of technology into teaching and learning.

The SAMR Model

The intent of this model (see Figure 9.3) created by Ruben Puentedora (2006) is to help educators consider how technology is being used in the classroom. It provides educators with an approach for reflecting on how technology is being used to enrich learning. Although the model may appear to be hierarchical, this is not the intent. What the model depicts is a range of how technology can be integrated into teaching and learning starting at the substitution level and moving to the modification level. At the substitution level, technology is being used in ways that brings about no functional change to the task being accomplished (e.g., taking notes).

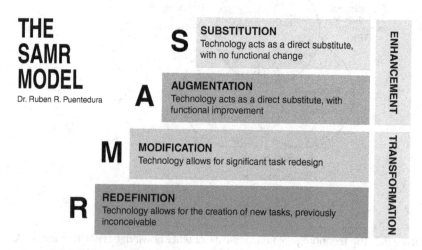

Figure 9.3 The SAMR Model, developed by Dr. Ruben Puentedora

At the modification level, technology is being used in ways that necessarily change the way a task can be accomplished. Helping education consider how technology can be integrated into teaching and learning in order to redefine the traditional learning environment is a primary outcome of this model.

Technology Integration Matrix

This model was developed to assist educators in evaluating technology integration in the classroom. According to the Florida Center for Instructional Technology (n.d.), "In contrast to other models for technology integration, the TIM is designed to evaluate a lesson, as opposed to rating a teacher or judging a discrete task" (para. 1). The Technology Integration Matrix is a combination of "characteristics of meaningful learning environments" (para. 1) that are "associated with five levels of technology integration: entry, adoption, adaptation, infusion, and transformation" (para. 1). By using the matrix, an educator can reflect on the pedagogy that is being used and how students are engaging with technology.

The ISTE Standards

The International Society for Technology in Education (ISTE) Standards—although not an integration model—provides structure for considering technology integration. There are five sets of standards and one set of competencies (for computer science). The five sets include standards for students, educators, education leaders, coaches, and computer science educators. The Standards for Students outline skills that when mastered lead to effective use of technology and abilities that help learners succeed in our contemporary society. The Standards for Educators outline skills that assist educators in effectively leveraging technology in their teaching and professional growth. Mastering these standards can provide educators with the skills and knowledge needed to create learning environments that empower their learners.

We are confident that you are already familiar with the student and educator standards. As a change agent, it is important that you are also familiar with the Standards for Coaches. ISTE indicates that the Standards for

Coaches describe the skills and knowledge that technology coaches need "to support their peers in becoming digital age educators" (ISTE, 2019a). The Standards for Coaches includes seven standards that are made up of 28 indicators. The Standards focus on coaches being a change agent, a connected learner, a collaborator, a learning designer, a professional learning facilitator, a data-driven decision maker, and a digital citizen advocate (ISTE, 2019b). We suggest that you strive to become competent with the indicators that make up the Standards for Coaches because the competence you gain will increase your ability to be an effective change agent.

 Point to Consider: Dissecting the ISTE Standards

All five sets of ISTE Standards follow a similar structure. You will be better able to help others meet the standards if you are aware of how they are structured. Each set of standards have higher level standards broken into indicators. The Standards for Coaches includes seven standards that are made up of 28 indicators. Let's take a look at one of the standards and one of its indicators. Standard 2 is titled Connected Learner and it has three indicators. This standard reads, "Coaches model the ISTE Standards for Students and the ISTE Standards for Educators, and identify ways to improve their coaching practice" (ISTE, 2019b). Indicator 2c of this standard indicates that technology coaches should be able to "Actively participate in professional learning networks to enhance coaching practice and keep current with emerging technology and innovations in pedagogy and the learning sciences" (ISTE, 2019b). To be competent with Standard 2, you would need to be able to demonstrate competence with indicator 2c and the other two indicators. We recommended that you become familiar with the Standards for Coaches (actually, all of the ISTE Standards) and strive to become competent with the indicators associated with this set of standards. You can start by reading through the indicators and assessing how competent you feel with the indicators. You can locate the ISTE Standards for Coaches at https://www.iste.org/standards/for-coaches. An updated version of these standards was released in October, 2019.

Our Framework for Considering Technology

We developed our framework because we often are asked—"How in the world can I understand and keep up with *all* of the technology that is out there?" Our answer is simple and may no doubt be comforting to many of you: Do not try! As educational technology experts, we, too, can get lost in the seemingly endless sea of technology. We realize that there is a vast amount of technology that can be used for teaching and learning. Being aware of all that is available and making sense of it can be overwhelming—especially with new technology popping up on what seems like a weekly basis. So, instead of trying to understand and keep up with all of the latest and greatest technology, we advocate that you follow an approach that allows you to find the technology—specifically, software—you need, when you need it. Following a well thought-out approach will allow you to make informed decisions without having to undertake the nearly impossible task of staying current with *all* technology.

 ## Point to Consider: Second-Level Digital Divide

We have no doubts that you are familiar with the term the digital divide. As a reminder, the digital divide refers to the gap between those who have access to digital technology and the Internet and those who do not. Are you aware of the term the *second digital divide?* This is an important concept for change agents to know. The second-level digital divide refers to the gap "between those people who are lost in the digital environment and those who have the skills to navigate efficiently and effectively through all the information now available to them through digital technologies" (OECD, 2011). Julie Reinhart, Earl Thomas, and Jeanne Toriskie (2011) write about this idea in regard to K-12 teaching and learning. They indicate that the second-level digital divide has to do with how technology is being used rather than access to technology. They state that educators who do not know how to effectively use technology for teaching and learning bring about a second-level digital divide in their classrooms because although their learners may have access to technology, the learners lack the opportunities to use technology in meaningful ways. Reinhart et al. provide suggestions for dealing with the second-level digital divide. One suggestion is for teachers to have access to technology specialists who can provide training, modeling, and guidance to help educators effectively use technology in the classroom.

The primary goal of our approach is to help educators build confidence in being able to understand and select technology that supports teaching and learning that fosters contemporary skills no matter what the grade level, content, or instructional objectives. Our approach is not about prescribing how and when you should use technology. Instead, we provide guidance on how to consider and reflect on technology use for teaching and learning that helps meet the needs of your learners. Our approach includes three elements. These three elements work together to help change agents make informed decisions about the technology used in the learning environment. Having an approach will allow you, as a change agent, to pass along this approach so others can make their own informed decisions.

The first element in our approach includes a chart that organizes software into categories based on the contemporary skills of critical thinking, communication, collaboration, and creativity (the 4 Cs). Change agents can use the chart to select software they will integrate into instruction. The chart can be used as a framework for thinking about new software that educators discover. The second element in our approach is a table that helps educators consider what they are doing instructionally in the classroom. In considering what is done instructionally, educators are able to clearly identify what type of software will best meet instructional outcomes. The third element is a set of questions to help determine whether a particular piece of software chosen is the most appropriate given the stated instructional purpose. As mentioned, the ultimate outcomes of following this approach are to help make sense of the software available and then to determine what is the best software to use in a specific teaching and learning situation.

Key Considerations

We feel it is important to mention a few key ideas before we move into the discussion of the three elements:

- Our attempt to make sense of the software that learners and educators have available is not something that is unique. This type of activity has been going on for many years. As such, there are a variety of approaches that have been developed that attempt to do what we have done. We appreciate many of them, and many of them sparked our thinking as we developed our own approach. Our approach focuses on software rather than hardware. We have consciously made this decision because we believe that *most* of the decisions that educators make about the use of technology focus on the software they and their learners will use rather than hardware. This is not to minimize the importance of hardware, because it is obvious that hardware is important.

- Any attempt to design and create an organizational scheme—especially one based on content that is dynamic and continuously evolving like technology—can be problematic if not carefully thought out. One major issue is that the organizational scheme can become quickly outdated. Our organizational scheme has held up and will continue to hold up over time because it is organized around contemporary skills—the 4 Cs.

- It is inevitable that the specific technology included in any organizational scheme can also become quickly outdated due to how rapidly technology evolves. It is important to recognize that at a specific moment in time, the technology being organized and described was current. This is true with the software we include in this chapter. At the time the book was written, we included software that was alive and well (and ones we believed would continue to be). Some of these may, however, no longer exist. We really hope this is not the case because we regularly use what is included in the chapter.

Element One: Organizing Technology

We stated earlier in the chapter that our attempt to organize technology is not the first one to have ever been done, nor the last. This type of activity has been going on for years. When looking at the literature, you can find a number of different approaches ranging from grouping educational software according to their instructional purpose such as tutorial, exploratory, application, and communication (Means et al., 1993), to grouping based on interactions the software allows, such as learner with an expert, learner with another learner, learner with content, and learner with a particular context (Culatta, 2009), to considering software based on the level to which the educator perceives the software provides opportunities for learners to meet learning goals (Kolb, 2011). Although each organizational scheme can provide some benefit, we feel that focusing on contemporary skills is a more useful approach. Focusing on the contemporary skill that can be developed by the software makes our approach enduring. It places the focus on skills rather than on the functionality of the software or the assessment of the usefulness of the software. It also helps educators focus on an expectation of the *Common Core State Standards*, which is the meaningful integration of technology and contemporary skills with content.

 Point to Consider: What About Hardware?

We do not want you to be left with the impression that hardware is not important. It is quite the opposite. Software and hardware go hand-in-hand. For software to meet its purpose, it must have hardware to run on. For hardware to serve its purpose, it needs software to run it. Hardware, therefore, is crucial for a contemporary educational environment, and it needs to be carefully considered. We have found, however, that most hardware decisions are not left to individual educators to make. In other words, the hardware we have access to in the classroom is often determined at the district level or through a school-wide committee. Educators' decisions primarily focus on the software that will be used with the hardware. Because of this, we focused on making sense of software and have not categorized hardware.

Using the Contemporary Skills Software Chart

Let's examine how the Contemporary Skills Software Chart (Table 9.2) can be used. Notice that the chart is divided into three columns. The first

Table 9.2 Contemporary Skills Software Chart

Contemporary Skill	Software Categories	Software Examples	
Creativity	Audio and video creation	• Adobe Spark Video • Animoto® • Apple Clips • Audacity®	• GarageBand® • iMovie® • MovieMaker® • WeVideo
	Digital storytelling	• Adobe Spark Page • Storybird™	
	Finding and sharing ideas	• Flipboard • Scoop.it	• Wakelet
	Image creation	• Adobe Spark Post • Canva • PicCollage	• Skitch • Sketchup™
	Image and photo sharing	• Flickr® • Google Photos	• Photobucket • Shutterfly
	Presentations	• Glogster© • Google Slides • Keynote • Knovio™	• MIcrosoft Sway • PowerPoint® • Prezi® • ThinkLink
	Screencasting	• Camtasia® • Explain Everything • iorad • Screencast-o-matic	• ScreenFlow® • Screenr™ • Screencastify
Critical thinking	Data collection and analysis tools	• Desmos • GeoGebra • Google Forms™	• Numbers • SurveyMonkey • Qualtrics
	Internet search tools	• Google Scholar™ • Google Advanced Search™	
	Polling and response software	• AnswerGarden • Crowdsignal • Google Form • GoSoapBox™	• Kahoot • PollEverywhere Quizziz
	Resource organization and sharing	• Diigo • Dropbox • Evernote • Pinterest™	

(continued)

Table 9.2 (Cont.)

Contemporary Skill	Software Categories	Software Examples	
	Visualization and concept mapping	• Bubbl.us • Popplet • Debategraph.org© • Gliffy© • Inspiration® and Inspiration Maps®	• Kidspiration and Kidspiration Maps • Mindmeister • Mind42 • Wordle™ • Word Clouds
Communication and collaboration	*Cloud-based storage and sharing*	• Dropbox® • Sugar Sync®	
	Collaborative document Development and sharing	• Google docs™ • Google Drive • Evernote®	• iCloud Sharing • LiveBinder™ • Office365
	Learning management systems	• Canvas® • PowerSchool Learning	• Moodle™ • Schoology
	Virtual bulletin boards	• Lino • Padlet	• Portaportal • Symbaloo©
	Virtual whiteboards	• AwwApp • Scribblar©	• Web Whiteboard • Ziteboard
	Blogs and micro-blogs	• Edublogs • Weebly	• Twitter • Wix • WordPress
	Live conversations	FaceTime™ Google Hangouts Meet	• Skype™ • Zoom™
	Discussions, threaded discussions, and audio discussions	• Flipgrid • Nabble • Peardeck • VoiceThread© • Voxer	
	Video sharing and viewing	• Discovery Education Streaming • TeacherTube®	• Vimeo© • YouTube™

column includes the contemporary skills of critical thinking, collaboration, communication, and creativity. The second column divides software into categories based on functionality, and the third column lists specific software that can be used in ways that promote the contemporary skill.

Let's assume you are interested in locating software that can help develop learner creativity. Locate *Creativity* in the left column. You can now locate the categories associated with the contemporary skill. Audio and Video Creation is listed as a category for *Creativity*. Under this category, teachers can find specific software that allows students to create and manipulate audio and video—Adobe Spark Video®, Audacity®, Garage Band®, iMovie®, and MovieMaker®. You can now choose specific software from this category that you and your learners could use. We realize that educators may not have access to or be familiar with the software listed. If this is the case, we suggest doing a web search to locate the software. Each piece of software listed has its own website where information about the software can be found, and in most cases, you can download the software for free or receive a trial version.

As you use the Contemporary Skills Software Chart (Figure 9.4), there are a few things to understand about the categories and software on the chart:

• The categories we use are ones that we have either created or adopted. There certainly could be additional categories; however, we use ones that make the most sense to us. Once you become more comfortable with technology, we encourage you to create your own categories or

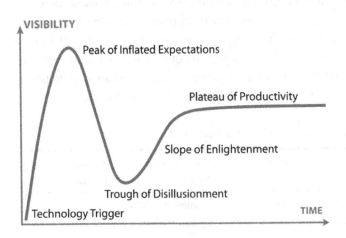

Figure 9.4 The Gartner Hype Cycle (2019)

modify the categories we have provided. This will help the chart be more meaningful and useful to you.

- The list of software we include is not exhaustive. We include software that we have used and continue to use. We realize that there are other excellent software that could be included. Again, we encourage you to include other software as you become familiar with software that we have not included.

- Some of the software we include could help foster more than one contemporary skill and could fit into multiple categories. We have categorized the software based on our own use. Please do not let our categorization limit how you and your learners use the software.

- Most of the software we have included can be used for free or for a low cost. Some of the tools require a monthly or yearly fee. Others require a one-time fee to purchase.

- Most of the software is cross-platform (e.g., iOS, OS, Windows, Android) that run through the Web. There are some, however, that are desktop based and will need to be located directly on a computer.

Element Two: Considering Your Instruction

Once you are comfortable with the process for making sense of the software that is available, you are in a solid position to consider how the software can fit into your unique teaching and learning environment and to help others do the same. We provide a framework—the Instructional Development Framework (Table 9.3)—that we believe is helpful in considering how software can help students meet instructional outcomes (i.e., content standards and learning objectives) and develop contemporary skills. This framework is the second element of our approach.

Table 9.3 Instructional Development Framework

Intended Learning Outcomes/ Objectives	Contemporary Skill(s)	Learning Activity and Software
Build on other's talk in conversations by linking their comments to the remarks of others	Communication Collaboration	

The Instructional Development Framework has three components that are included in a three-column chart. The first component is the learning outcomes educators want learners to meet. The contemporary skill or skills that educators are introducing or reinforcing with their learners is the second component. The third component is the software that can help learners meet the learning outcome and facilitate the development of the contemporary skill. Let's examine each of these three components by working through an example from a second grade classroom perspective.

The first column of the framework includes outcomes based on content standards, learning goals, or learning objectives. In essence, the learning outcomes are what learners should be able to do. We focus on the English Language Arts Common Core Standards. Specially, we will focus on Second Grade Standard 1 from the Speaking and Listening Standards for K-5 (http://www.corestandards.org/assets/CCSSI_ELA%20Standards.pdf). This standard indicates that second grade students, by the end of the year, should be able to "build on other's talk in conversations by linking their comments to the remarks of others" (p. 23). The learning activity (column 3) will be some form of a discussion (Table 9.4).

Element Three: Determining the Specific Software

At this point in the process, the final element includes selecting the specific software that will be integrated into instruction and then determining its appropriateness by asking a series of questions about the software. Let's continue with the second grade classroom example to examine how we suggest going about accomplishing element three of our approach. In the

Table 9.4 Instructional Development Framework: Learning Activity Included

Intended Learning Outcomes/ Objectives	Contemporary Skill(s)	Learning Activity and Software
Build on other's talk in conversations by linking their comments to the remarks of others	Communication Collaboration	Discussion

Table 9.5 Instructional Development Framework: Software Included

Intended Learning Outcomes/ Objectives	Contemporary Skill(s)	Learning Activity and Software
Build on other's talk in conversations by linking their comments to the remarks of others	Communication Collaboration	Discussion (activity) Software (Flipgrid)

example, we determined that having a discussion would be the learning activity used to help learners meet the intended learning outcome and to practice communication and collaboration skills. We then looked at the Contemporary Software Chart to determine what software would facilitate this type of learning activity. There were several specific software choices that were listed as options. We chose Flipgrid, the video-based discussion tool (Table 9.5).

We suggest that if an educator is completely unfamiliar with the software, the educator should answer the following questions about each software to determine which will be the best fit for helping meet the intended learning outcome. Educators have indicated that these questions have been helpful.

Q1. Do I understand the primary purpose of the software?

A1. Most software is designed to carry out a specific task. This does not mean it cannot be used for other tasks. However, it is important to understand what the software's purpose is. Take a look at the website associated with the software. You should be able to find a clear description of the software's purpose.

Q2. Do I have the required technical specifications to run this software? For example, is an Internet connection needed to run the software? Will it only run on the Apple® iOS or OS?

A2. Again, take a look at the software's website to determine this information.

Q3. Is the software affordable?

A3. Information about cost will be clearly listed on the software's website as well. Most software comes with a free-trial option that can be useful so you can try out the software to determine if it truly meets you and your learners' needs. Make sure you check to determine if there is an educational discount or price, or a volume discount.

Q4. What are the major barriers or issues I foresee with using the software? Will I be able to overcome these issues?

A4. The barriers or issues will vary greatly depending on the software and your school or district. It is difficult to anticipate all of them. Cost, access to websites where the software is located, downloading software, and installing software on computers or mobile devices you have access to are examples of barriers or issues you many have to address. The key here is to think about potential barriers, but more importantly determining the ways in which they can be overcome or worked around is what you need to consider. For example, are the barriers something you can overcome or will it require district or administrative support?

Q5. Do I have adequate time to learn how to use the software prior to implementation?

A5. An educator needs to realistically determine whether he or she could learn to use the software on his or her own and whether there is adequate time to do so. The best way to determine this is to try out the software. The educator should find out if there are online tutorials available. Most software have tutorials available on their website. Also, find out if the district office or county office provides training. If the software is one that many educators use, it is highly likely that someone has created resources that can be accessed online on how to use the software.

Q6. What type of training will I need to provide my learners so they learn how to use the software? Am I capable of providing this training?

A6. If you need to train your learners on how to use the software, this time needs to be factored into your instructional plans. One thing to remember is that even though you may not have familiarity with the software, your learners may have already experienced it in other environments, such as with other educators or as part of their nonacademic life.

The information an educator gathers from asking these questions will help determine the best software choice for what the educator is trying to accomplish instructionally. If the educator answers the majority of the questions with a *yes*, then we believe the educator has selected appropriate software that will put the educator in a solid position to effectively integrate the software. On the other hand, if a majority of the questions were answered with a *no*, the software might not be the most appropriate choice. We do not want to suggest, however, that an educator completely avoids software that they are not familiar with using.

Research to Consider: Barriers to Technology Integration

Peggy Ertmer (1999) wrote a seminal article about the barriers educators face in integrating technology into their practice. In the article, *Addressing First- and Second-Order Barriers to Change: Strategies for Technology Integration,* Ertmer discussed extrinsic issues (first-order barriers) and intrinsic issues (second-order barriers). Extrinsic issues focus on obstacles that are typically outside of an educator's control such as equipment, time, training, and support. Intrinsic issues are those that "are typically rooted in teachers' underlying beliefs about teaching and learning" (p. 51). Ertmer discusses strategies for dealing with these issues—developing a vision, collaboration, modeling, and reflecting. As change agents, this is a must read. This will provide you with an overall understanding of barriers educators face and strategies for dealing with these issues. Ertmer has published other research that discusses additional barriers related to teachers' pedagogical beliefs. The article, *Teacher Pedagogical Beliefs: The Final Frontier in Our Quest for Technology Integration?* (2005), is another one we recommend change agents read.

Ertmer, P. A. (1999). Addressing first-and second-order barriers to change: Strategies for technology integration. *Educational Technology Research and Development, 47*(4), 47–61.

Ertmer, P. A. (2005). Teacher pedagogical beliefs: The final frontier in our quest for technology integration? *Educational Technology Research and Development, 53*(4), 25–39.

Point to Consider: Who Makes the Decisions About Technology Policy?

As a change agent, it is important to understand how decisions about technology policy are made in your school and district. Often, policy decisions are made by the administration or in consultation with information technology personnel with little to no involvement from educators or other stakeholders. We do not support this approach. We advocate for a shared process for developing technology policy. Without a shared decision-making process, policies can be developed and put in place that severely (and often unnecessarily) affect the access and use of technology for teaching and learning. We have documented (Robinson, Brown, & Green, 2010) numerous instances where well-intentioned policy was made without consultations with educators that ended up leading to unintended and unnecessary consequences (e.g., banning of educational apps or websites).

The most effective approach we have found in our experience is one where all stakeholders are represented and have a voice. Input is needed from a wide-range of viewpoints if policy is to be inclusive. We understand that school and district dynamics vary. As such, we caution you with how you approach this. Do investigate how policy is made. Do push to be involved. Do push to have a shared process that is inclusive of stakeholders. Do, however, know that you could get push-back and come up against a brick wall. If you are interested in a resource that describes a shared process for technology decision-making, we suggest the book, *Securing the Connected Classroom: Technology Planning to Keep Students Safe* (Brown & Green, 2014).

 ## Staying Current with Educational Technology

We mentioned in the previous section that it can be difficult if not impossible to stay current with the vast amount of available technology that can be used for teaching and learning. Despite this difficulty, as change agents we should still attempt to maintain a solid understanding of the current trends and issues in educational technology because we are often sought out for advice and our opinions. We also need to be able to have an understanding of the trends and issues so we can anticipate how the educators and learners we support could be affected. The better our knowledge is, the more prepared we will be to initiate and lead change and innovation adoption. Admittedly, we do not believe we have the definitive solution for staying current, but we can, however, share the resources we draw from on a regular basis. These resources include podcasts, professional journals, annual reports, popular press and media outlets, social media, professional conferences, professional learning communities, and un-conferences (e.g., EdCamp). We debated whether to provide specific examples of these resources in the book. We decided to point you to our website (http:// thepurposeframework.com/) where we maintain an updated list rather than risk including resources in the book that might no longer exist when you are reading this book. We encourage you to share with us the resources that you use that are not on our site.

 ## Point to Consider: The Gartner Hype Cycle

One resource that we believe all change agents should be aware of is the Gartner Hype Cycle. This tool was developed to show how various technologies or applications go through the maturation process and adoption. This is represented graphically (see Figure 9.4). A technology or application begins with some form of trigger (e.g., media buzz) that brings attention to it. As it gains traction and more people start to use it, it often reaches the Peak of Inflated Expectations. At some point, individuals often become disillusioned with it and it begins to lose its value as its capabilities become overinflated. When this occurs, fewer people use the technology or application and it slips into the Trough of Disillusionment. The Slope of Enlightenment is when the technology or application is either improved or people start to determine more effective ways to use it. If enough people are using the technology or application effectively and it becomes part of their practice (i.e., it has been adopted), the technology or application will reach the Plateau of Productivity. It is important to note that there is no typical time period that all technology or applications go through the Hype Cycle. The movement through the cycle varies. It is also important to note that not all technology or applications make it through all five phases. Those that do are typically adopted into long-term practice.

Annually, Gartner comes out with various hype cycles. Two that we find informative are emerging technologies and technologies in education. You can find these on their website at https://www.gartner.com/en/research/methodologies/gartner-hype-cycle.

It is also important to note that the Hype Cycle has been criticized by some for its alleged lack of data to support the movement of a technology or application through the cycle. Despite this critique, we believe the Hype Cycle has value in providing a view of emerging technologies and applications—what is "hot" and where they are being viewed on the cycle (according to the Gartner Research Group, 2019).

 ## Jody's Perspective from the Trenches: Integration Models

When teachers first received devices in my district, they attended 3 days of formal professional learning with me. I introduced and discussed different integration models during the three PD days. The model that was embraced the most by teachers was the SAMR Model. It provided them with a visual construct for what technology integration could look like in the classroom, and it was an easy entry point for me to help teachers understand different ways technology could be used in the classroom. We focused our approach on asking ourselves what students were doing with the tech in order to help us move away from a teacher-centered approach to using technology in the classroom. I was also careful to point out to teachers that SAMR was more of a lens or an anchor for them to begin asking themselves questions about what they were doing with technology in the classroom and not a "ladder," as it is sometimes referred that they needed to climb in order to "do integration correctly." As teachers became more comfortable having technology in their classrooms and planning lessons that integrate technology, we were able to start having deeper conversations around the ISTE standards and how those standards influence the work we do with students in the classroom.

Instructional Practices

Computer-based technology began to be a fixture in PK-12 education in the 1970s. The focus at that time was primarily on learning *about* technology and how it worked. Technology availability in classrooms was relatively limited. As technology developed during the 1980s and became more available, the focus shifted in the 1990s to learning *from* technology. Learners began using technology as tools to learn content and practice skills. By the start of the 21st century, with the increased capabilities of and access to technology (including access to the Internet), there was another shift—a shift to learning *with* technology. Technology became a tool that supported learners not only in their learning of content, but also with their development of contemporary skills (e.g., critical thinking, collaboration). With two decades of the 21st century past, we are now at a time when another shift is occurring.

Technology is becoming ubiquitous in schools. We concede that some schools have more access to technology than others. Technology, however, is widely available (and becoming more so) to educators and learners—as is access to the Internet. According to the *2019 State of the States* report (Education Superhighway, 2019), 99% of schools have access to the Internet. With this increased access in schools to the Internet and increasingly more sophisticated technology coupled with relatively high levels of personal access our learners have to technology, a shift in how technology is being used for learning is under way. We describe this shift as learning anytime, anywhere *through* technology (Green & Donovan, 2018). We wrote in 2018 that PK-12 education "is in a position for this shift to occur due to several reasons—the ubiquitous nature of technology, the continued rapid advancements in technology, the access to robust networked computer environments, the promising practices that effectively integrate technology" (Green & Donovan, 2018, p. 243). In addition to these reasons, "the increase in research that is informing our understanding of how technology can affect student learning, and the characteristics and dispositions of the iMakers" (Green & Donovan, 2018, p. 243) are helping bring about this shift to learning anytime, anywhere through technology. Learning anytime, anywhere through technology is characterized by the use of technology to provide opportunities in and outside of school for learners to engage in learner-centered learning.

What is involved in learner-centered learning? Think back to Chapter 8 when we discussed the iMakers. We discussed eight characteristics that described how they approach and prefer to engage in learning. The iMakers want to be involved in:

making their learning environments,

making play and experimentation part of learning,

making through do-it-yourself and do-it-with-others projects,

making learning anywhere, anytime,

making through remixing and mash-ups,

making sense of change and innovation,

making their voices heard, and

making connections to communities (Green & Donovan, 2018).

A few key elements run through this list that are important to consider. iMakers want to be actively involved in all aspects of their learning. They want learning to include social elements. They want to be makers—this means that they have the desire to design, create, experiment, and invent. They want opportunities for learning outside of the traditional classroom.

We believe that the affordances of technology make it possible to design and facilitate teaching and learning that meets these preferences. We know, as you do, that technology does not intrinsically have magical powers. Without research-supported practices facilitated by skilled educators, technology has and will always have its limitations. Technology, however, in the hands of skilled educators who are using research-supported practices can produce engaging and high-impact learning opportunities for their learners.

Our goal for this chapter is to share 10 promising instructional practices that can support student learning anytime, anywhere through technology. Although the research may be mixed about these practices, there is evidence (strong evidence with some) that they hold potential for improving learning outcomes and helping learners gain contemporary skills they need to be successful during PK-12 and beyond. These instructional practices are influencing how educators engage their learners in the learning process. Although it is beyond the scope of this chapter to provide an analysis of the research on each instructional practice, what we have provided are concise descriptions of the instructional practices.

We have no doubts that you are familiar with these instructional practices and have most likely used at least one of them. We want you to keep in mind the outcome of this chapter as you read the descriptions. The outcome is for you to gain an awareness and understanding of them—it is not about gaining the necessary skills to use these instructional practices. As change agents, it is important that we clearly understand what these promising instructional practices are and what they were designed to do. We must be able to accurately define and describe them if we are going to provide support to educators who are infusing technology with these instructional practices.

 # Point to Consider: Instructional Practices? Methods? Models? Strategies? Techniques?

There are several terms that are used in PK-12 that describe approaches that we use as educators to facilitate teaching and learning. The terms that quickly come to mind are instructional methods, instructional models, instructional practices, instructional strategies, and instructional techniques. Although you can find specific definitions for these terms, we have observed that there is variation with and disagreement about these definitions. This has led to the terms being used interchangeably, and we believe incorrectly at times. We use the term instructional practices in this chapter as an umbrella term that includes various elements dealing with how educators approach facilitating teaching and learning. The terms we listed above (e.g., instructional models, instructional techniques) would fit under instructional practices. We purposefully used this term because of the different approaches we included.

A useful perspective that we often share comes from Barrie Bennett (2018), who focused on the term instructional methods. He has broken instructional methods into three categories—instructional skills, tactics, and instructional strategies. Instructional skills are "simple or less complex" (p. 437) methods such as "Framing Questions, Using Wait Time, Sharing the Objective and Purpose of the Lesson, Responding to an Incorrect Response, and Suspending Judgement" (p. 437). Bennett indicated that tactics are more complex methods than instructional skills and typically have a higher effect size. He indicated that there are likely at least 250 instructional tactics (e.g., Think Pair Share, Venn Diagrams, Brainstorming). Instructional strategies "are the most complex and provide the most powerful effects" (p. 437). Bennett included Concept Attainment, Group Investigation, and Concept Mapping as examples of instructional Strategies.

As a change agent, it is important for us to be clear with the terms we use. We are not advocating that you follow our perspective or Bennett's, but we do, however, want you to be aware of them. Whatever perspective you use, be clear with what you mean when you use these terms, and be sure you have clarity with how others are using them.

Blended Learning. The blended learning model is an approach to teaching and learning that includes a mixture of traditional face-to-face instruction and online (Internet-based) instruction. The Christensen Institute (2016) indicates that, "Blended learning involves leveraging the Internet to afford each student a more personalized learning experience, including increased student control over the time, place, path, and/or pace of learning" (para. 1). The ability for learners to have control of their learning can lead to a personalized learning experience that includes enrichment and remediation opportunities. Blended learning can provide educators with increased time to engage with learners in small group instruction. It can also provide opportunities for learners to learn from and with their peers (Istance & Paniagua, 2019; Murphy et al., 2014).

According to the U.S. Office of Educational Technology (2016), blended learning often leads to a "reconfiguration of the physical learning space to facilitate learning activities, providing a variety of technology-enabled learning zones optimized for collaboration, informal learning, and individual-focused study" (p. 8). It is important to note that there are different configurations of blended learning. Blending learning can look different. The Christensen Institute (2016) identified four configurations: Rotation model, Flex model, A-la Carte model, and Enriched Virtual model.

 Point to Consider: Computational Thinking

With the push in PK-12 for coding and computer programming, an area that is receiving a great deal of attention is computational thinking. You need to be aware that there are a number of definitions for computational thinking. At a foundational level, computational thinking is the ability to use problem-solving processes. Often, this includes the use of computer-based technology. Although computational thinking has often been associated with computer science and the use of computer-based technology, the skills involved in computational thinking cut across all disciplines and content areas. These skills are abstraction, algorithm design, decomposition, and pattern recognition. As change agents, we should be advocating for these skills to be used throughout the curriculum in all grade levels.

To read more about computational thinking and about how International Society for Technology in Education (ISTE) view competencies related to computational thinking, we suggest you visit https://www.iste.org/standards/computational-thinking

Bring Your Own Device (BYOD) or Bring Your Own Technology (BYOT). The BYOD or BYOT approach in PK-12 has been a by-product of the one device per student (1:1) model that has been implemented in numerous schools and districts. As schools and districts struggle to provide learners with consistent access to updated devices, some have allowed learners to bring their own personal mobile devices to school. Granted, there are a number of documented challenges associated with BYOD or BYOT. Despite the challenges, BYOD or BYOT can bring about many important benefits for learners—an increase in engagement, more control over learning opportunities, the development of digital and information literacies, opportunities for collaboration and communication, and the development of social and interpersonal skills (Clifford, 2012; Cristol & Gimbert, 2013; Engle & Green, 2011; Parsons & Adhikari, 2016).

Cloud-Based Learning. Cloud-based learning refers to teaching and learning that takes place in a cloud-computing environment. Mell and Grance (2011) wrote that, "Cloud computing is a model for enabling ubiquitous, convenient, on-demand, network access to a shared pool of configurable computing resources (e.g., networks, servers, storage, applications, and services) that can be rapidly provisioned and released with minimal management effort or service provider interaction" (p. 2). What does this mean? Cloud computing (or the Cloud) provides educators and learners with access through various Internet-connected devices to software, file storage, collaborative workspaces, and tools. This allows learners to engage in learning anytime and anywhere. Learners do not have to be bound by place, space, or time to communicate, collaborate, and engage with other learners, educators, and experts. Google Suite for Education is an example of a popular technology that allows cloud-based learning.

Flipped Learning. The Flipped Learning Network (2014) described Flipped Learning as "a pedagogical approach in which direct instruction moves from the group learning space to the individual learning space, and the resulting group space is transformed into a dynamic, interactive learning environment where the educator guides students as they apply concepts and engage creatively in the subject matter" (p. 1). Flipped Learning has learners engage with content outside of the typical class structure through a variety of media such as audio, video, and Web-based and print-based resources to allow in-class time to be more personalized through individual activities, small group instruction, one-on-one instruction, peer-to-peer interactions, and learner directed activities. We suggest reading the resource (see References) that the Flipped Learning Network created that describes the four pillars of Flipped Learning—flexible environment, learning culture, intentional content, and professional educator. They make a clear distinction between a Flipped Classroom and Flipped Learning. They indicate that a Flipped Classroom does not necessarily lead to Flipped Learning. They indicate that, "Many teachers may already flip their classes by having students read text outside of class, watch supplemental videos, or solve additional problems, but to engage in Flipped Learning, teachers must incorporate the following four pillars into their practice" (p. 1).

Gamification and Game-Based Learning. It is important to understand that gamification and game-based learning are not the same. Gamification is the use of game elements in a non-game setting such as a PK-12 classroom. Lee and Hammer (2011) indicate that, "Gamification can motivate students to engage in the classroom, give teachers better tools to guide and reward students, and get students to bring their full selves to the pursuit of learning. It can show them the ways that education can be a joyful experience, and the blurring of boundaries between informal and formal learning can inspire students to learn in lifewide, lifelong, and lifedeep ways" (p. 4). Digital badges, point systems, and leaderboards are elements often used in gamification. Game-based learning on the other hand, "involves designing learning activities so that game characteristics and game principles inhere within the learning activities themselves" (Centre for Teaching Excellence, n.d., para. 4). It is the use of actual games (i.e., Oregon Trail, Stock Market) to help students meet learning outcomes. The Centre for Teaching and Learning at the University of Waterloo (n.d.) states, "In short, gamification applies game elements or a game framework to existing learning activities; game-based learning designs learning activities that are intrinsically game-like" (p. 5).

Maker Spaces. We discussed in Chapter 8 that "The maker movement refers broadly to the growing number of people who are engaged in the creative production of artifacts in their daily lives and who find physical and digital forums to share their process and products with others" (Halverson & Sheridan 2014, p. 496).

Maker spaces allow individuals to engage in practices and processes that allow them to design and create products that have personal meaning. Maker spaces are the physical locations where learners are able to work on their own (the Do It Yourself [DIY] approach) or work collaboratively with others (the Do It With Others [DOWO] approach). In PK-12 schools, most maker spaces are located within a classroom where learners have access to a combination of digital and analog resources. These spaces allow learners to create products and to share their products along with the processes they used in creating them.

Online Learning and Online Distance Education. Although these two instructional practices share similarities, they have a major difference—when and how interactions take place. Online learning is teaching and learning that is facilitated through the Internet. This can take place in or out of the classroom. Online distance education is also teaching and learning that is delivered through the Internet where the interactions among learners and educators and learners and learners are separated by time, location, or both. Although both online learning and online distance education are facilitated through the Internet (i.e., online) and both could occur in the classroom, online distance education involves learners engaging with others who are located elsewhere (i.e., that is, from a distance). This is the major difference. As change agents, it is important to understand this difference. It is also important to understand that an online distance education learning activity can take place in a face-to-face classroom. An example would be inviting a guest speaker into the classroom using a videoconferencing tool like Zoom. This is online distance education because the learners and the expert are not physically in the same location. Online distance education can include learning activities like this or it can refer to a completely online course or school. Finally, it is important to understand the popularity of online distance education in PK-12. According to the Evergreen Education Group (2019), state virtual schools served 420,000 students and approached " one million supplemental online course enrollments in 23 states during the 2016–17 fiscal year" (p. 18).

Open Educational Resources (OER). A definition of OER that we often share comes from the Hewlett Foundation (2016). They write that,

"OER are teaching, learning, and research resources that reside in the public domain or have been released under an intellectual property license that permits their free use and re-purposing by others" (para. 2). OER can range from an entire book to a portion of an online course to a handout. We (Green & Brown, 2018) indicated that, "OER provides educators and students with access to many high quality materials and resources that can be modified to meet specific teaching and learning needs because they are typically digital and free of intellectual property licenses" (p. 247). Despite the appeal of OER, there are drawbacks. One of the major drawbacks is the lack of vetting of many OER. Although there are high-quality OER, there are equally as many poorly designed OER.

Personalized Learning. Personalized learning is often misunderstood. Typically, it is equated with self-paced, individualized learning that can be differentiated and facilitated using technology. Although these could be elements of personalized learning, this description does not give an accurate description of what personalized learning is. Learners engaging in personalized learning demonstrate mastery of content and skills in a competency-based system. Learners are actively involved in setting goals that are related to competencies. Andrew Miller (2019) wrote that, "Instead of students working at their own pace on completely self-imposed goals, they are involved in the planning and learning process as agents in that learning" (para. 14). Learners are also actively involved in choosing their resources, the approaches to how they engage in learning, and where they choose to engage in this learning. Miller also writes that learners "connect their learning to their interests and passions, and are allowed voice and choice in how they are assessed. Personalized learning involves self-pacing, but what's more important is that it connects learning to students' passions" (para. 15).

Project-Based Learning. The Buck Institute for Education (2019) describes project-based learning as "a teaching method in which students learn by actively engaging in real-world and personally meaningful projects" (para. 1). The 2015 National Educational Technology Plan (U.S. Office of Education, Office of Educational Technology, 2016) indicated that, project-based learning "takes place in the context of authentic problems, continues across time, and brings in knowledge from many subjects" (p. 11). Project-based learning when implemented effectively helps learners build contemporary skills that include "creativity, collaboration, and leadership, and engages them in complex, real-world challenges that help them meet expectations for critical thinking" (p. 11). It is important to note that project-based learning and problem-based learning are not the same, although they have similar elements. The Center for Teaching Innovation at Cornell University indicates that, "Problem-based learning (PBL) is a student-centered approach in which students learn about a subject by working in groups to solve an open-ended problem. This problem is what drives the motivation and the learning" (para. 1).

Universal Design for Learning. Universal Design for Learning (UDL) is an approach to designing and delivering learning experiences based on principles grounded in research from the learning sciences on how the brain works and how individuals learn. The goal of UDL is to provide all learners with opportunities for learning that are equitable and that accommodate learning differences to eliminate barriers that impede learning (Rose & Meyer, 2002). The three principles of UDL are to provide learners with (1) multiple means of engagement, (2) multiple means of representation, and (3) multiple means of action and expression (CAST, Inc., 2019).

 Point to Consider: The Truth Is Out There—Understand the Theory and Research

We have witnessed through the years a number of instructional practices (and technologies) that have spread with abandon throughout PK-12. We have observed as the instructional practice was pushed by eduevangelists and edulebrities touting its success in engaging learners or improving learner achievement. Often, the only evidence given is that it has worked for them. We've observed as the excitement generated from educators moved the instructional practice up the Gartner Hype Cycle (see Point to Consider: Gartner Hype Cycle) to the Peak of Inflated Expectations only to drop into the Trough of Disillusionment once educators found that the instructional practice did not meet the touted outcomes. We've seen this happen many times, and we might have even been caught up in this excitement.

Although there is a need for those who challenge boundaries, introduce new innovations, and generate excitement, we need to approach with a reasoned course of action what is being pushed. Healthy skepticism is a must. We should do our homework to determine the theory and the research that support the instructional practices. We should ask questions.

As Fox Mulder stated, "The truth is out there." We apologize for the corny X-Files reference, but do not miss our point. It is important to understand for yourself why an instructional practice works (or doesn't) and what theory and research supports it. As change agents, we need to have the "truth" so we can share this with others who may get swept away by the cult of personality.

Key Points From Part II: The How of Educational Change and Innovation Adoption—Learners, Technology, and Instructional Practices

Let's Review!

- We look at teaching and learning from an ecological perspective in order to better understand how the interconnected components fit together and influence each other (Chapter 6).
- Educator self-efficacy and collective educator efficacy has a tremendous influence on the achievement of learners (Chapter 7).
- There are a number of perspectives that describe PK-12 learners (Chapter 8).
- Our perspective, the iMakers, is based on the maker mindset, which influences how they prefer to engage in learning (Chapter 8).

- There are nine characteristics of the iMakers, they reflect how they prefer to engage in learning (Chapter 8).

- Technology integration models are designed to help educators consider how to approach integrating technology into teaching and learning (Chapter 8).

- There are approaches to help educator determine what technology to use to help learners meet specific learning outcomes (Chapter 9).

- Staying current with trends and issues in educational technology is possible by following a systematic approach (Chapter 9).

- There is a shift from using learning *with* technology to learning anytime, anywhere *through* technology (Chapter 10).

- There are a number of research-based instructional practices that support learning anytime, anywhere *through* technology (Chapter 10).

Let's Explore and Practice

If you'd like to explore and practice with the concepts and ideas we included in Part II, we've provided a few activities that can help you delve into them.

1. Reflect on the concept of collective teacher efficacy. How might you help increase the collective teacher efficacy at your school or a school you support? We've provided some resources you can explore in the "Digging Deeper" section.

2. What software would you add to the Contemporary Skills Chart that we provided in Chapter 9? How might you reorganize this chart?

3. If you were asked to give a presentation to parents on how the learners we have in PK-12 schools prefer to learn, what ideas would you share?

4. After reading the data, we shared about the level of personal access learners have to technology, how might this information

help you and your colleagues approach the integration of technology in your teaching?

5. Consider the instructional practices discussed in Chapter 10. Is there one that you have not used? We encourage you to take some time to explore the instructional practice. Read the research and theory that support it. Ask your colleagues about the instructional practice. Search through social media to find other change agents who have used the instructional practice. Try it out with your learners.

Digging Deeper Into Learners, Technology, and Instructional Practices

We've provided some resources that you can explore if you would like to dig deeper into learners, technology, and instructional practices. The resources are websites, books, and articles that we have found extremely helpful in our understanding, development, and growth.

- **Annual Reports, Educational Statistics, and Research Reports**

  - EDUCAUSE. Provides access to the Horizon Report—an annual report that focuses on trends and issues in educational technology in K-12 and higher education. https://library.educause.edu/

  - National Center for Educational Statistics. website with data on access, demographics, and everything you need to know about the state of education. https://nces.ed.gov/

  - Pew Research Center. Research reports are provided on many issues (e.g., digital divide) related to PK-12 education. The Pew Internet Research on the Internet and technology includes reports focusing on technology use that are informative to educators. https://www.pewresearch.org/

  - Project Tomorrow. Annual reports on learner, educator, administrator, and parent perceptions of and use of technology for teaching and learning. https://tomorrow.org/

  - Regional Educational Laboratory Program. A U.S. government program that provides support for research on educational issues and policies. https://ies.ed.gov/ncee/edlabs/

- **Collective Teacher Efficacy**
  - Blog post by Jenny Donohoo. https://thelearningexchange.ca/collective-teacher-efficacy/
- **Instructional Practices and Resources**
  - Association of Educational Communications and Technologies (AECT). A professional organization focusing on improving learning and human performance. http://aect.org /
  - The Christensen Institute—Blended Learning. https://www.christenseninstitute.org/blended-learning/
  - The Flipped Learning Network resources. https://flippedlearning.org/ and https://flglobal.org/
  - A Canadian government sponsored website with resources on instructional practices to engage learners. https://thelearningexchange.ca/
  - A seminal book on research-based instructional models—*Models of Teaching* by Bruce Joyce, Marsha Weil, and Emily Calhoun.
  - John Hattie's website on Visible Learning: What Works Best for Learning. https://visible-learning.org/
  - MERLOT. A curated resource for OER primarily focused on higher education. http://merlot.org/
- **Technology Integration Models and Standards**
  - Aurora Institute (formerly INACOL). https://www.inacol.org/
  - Dr. Puentedura's blog (SAMR Model). http://hippasus.com/blog/archives/227
  - Dr. Puentedura speaks about applying SAMR. https://youtu.be/ZQTx2UQQvbU
  - ISTE. https://www.iste.org/
  - Technology Integration Matrix. https://fcit.usf.edu/matrix/
  - TPACK website. http://tpack.org/

PART III

The What of Educational Change and Innovation Adoption: The PURPOSE Framework

> When large numbers of people have a deeply understood sense of what needs to be done—and see their part in achieving that purpose—coherence emerges and powerful things happen.
>
> —Michael Fullan (2013, p. 77)

Let's review in case you have started with Part III. The *why* of educational change was the focus of Part I. We encouraged you to examine your why—the beliefs and purpose you hold as a change agent. We shared our why. We discussed that as educational technology change agents we believe that digital technology can be integrated in equitable and inclusive ways to improve educational experiences for all learners. We indicated that our *why*—through our *how*—manifests into our *what* of helping change agents gain the knowledge and skills they need to lead change and innovation adoption in schools. We described that we approach our purpose (our why) through the lens of educational change and innovation adoption, which helps us make sense of events, people, and the systems and structures that we work with. We discussed tenets of change along with three perspectives on educational change and innovation adoption. Part II focused on *how*—the actions that you take to realize your *why*. We discussed how our actions as educators directly influence our learners' performance. We shared that we look at teaching and learning through an ecological perspective, which influences how we approach categorizing our actions. We described that our actions fall into three categories: K-12 learners, technology, and instructional practices. Our actions focus on these areas because they are the ones that we have the most control over as educators.

Part III focuses on the *what*—the results of actions. To reach our what, we use our PURPOSE Framework, a process we use as educational technology change agents when we work with schools, districts, and teacher education programs as they engage in the change process and innovation adoption initiatives. The framework is a tool that you as a change agent can use as you lead the process of change and innovation adoption. Our primary goal of Part III is to provide a detailed step-by-step description of the PURPOSE Framework, so you may use it to facilitate change in your educational environment. Although the change we typically concentrate on when using the PURPOSE Framework is the use of technology to bring about digital-age learning, the framework works with other types of change.

We recommend that you sequentially follow the steps outlined in the framework. We understand, however, that this may not be the best approach for your unique situation. You may be well into the change process or you may be faced with circumstances that prevent you from completing the steps in order. Whatever your situation is, we suggest that you explore what is involved in each step to gain an overall understanding of the PURPOSE Framework. This understanding will help you determine what tasks you may have already completed, what tasks you need to complete next, or what tasks you possibly have overlooked.

Self-Reflection

As you read Part III, it is important to consider that as a change agent you need to be flexible and open-minded. We provide four self-reflection questions as a way to examine your biases. Awareness of your personal biases about change, the innovation being adopted, and about those you are asking to adopt the innovation will better equip you to successfully facilitate the change process and innovation adoption.

We suggest that you consider the following statements before you begin reading Part III.

1. How do you feel about change? How do you deal with it?
2. How often do you judge your colleague's attitude toward technology use for teaching and learning?
3. How patient are you with individuals who do not embrace change?
4. How would you answer the five questions Rogers suggests we ask ourselves about an innovation before it is adopted (see Chapter 5)?

Part III Objectives

We have outlined four outcomes to guide your reading of Part III. After reading Part III, *The What of Educational Change and Innovation Adoption*, you will be able to:

1. identify steps necessary to facilitate change and innovation adoption,
2. facilitate sustained innovation adoption in your unique environment, and
3. confidently describe yourself as a change agent.

An Overview of the PURPOSE Framework

We indicated in the opening that our purpose drives our actions. Our actions help us realize our *what* of helping change agents like you gain the knowledge and skills needed to lead change and innovation adoption in schools. We approach our actions through the lens of educational change and innovation adoption, which helps us make sense of events, people, and the systems and structures that we work with. As a result of years working as educational change agents using the lens of educational change and innovation adoption, we developed the PURPOSE Framework—a process for facilitating change and the adoption of an innovation. The framework can be used as a guide for initiating, implementing, and institutionalizing change. This framework is our *what* that will help you successfully approach and lead change in your environment.

PURPOSE is an acronym that stands for the main outcomes of the seven phases that make up the framework:

Planning

Understanding

Researching

Preparing

Operationalizing

Sustaining

Evaluating

Each phase includes multiple steps. Figure 11.1 depicts the PURPOSE Framework linearly to provide an overview of the phases along with their

P *Planning*	U *Understanding*	R *Researching*	P *Preparing*	O *Operationalizing*	S *Sustaining*	E *Evaluating*
Describing the adoption process, intended outcomes, and sources of change	Knowing the innovation and knowing the people you are asking to change	Becoming an informed change agent by learning about the concerns and perspectives of others	Conducting professional development and getting ready to implement	Implementing the innovation and supporting the innovation adopters	Continuing support for innovation adoption and looking ahead	Determining impact and getting ready to prepare again

Figure 11.1 The PURPOSE framework.

major outcomes. In actuality, the implementation of the phases is recursive. Phases will need to be revisited as you go through the framework, and often, you will work on multiple steps at one time.

The remaining chapters of Part III are devoted to describing and outlining each phase. The chapters begin with an overall description of the phase that includes the theoretical background for the phase being described. Next, the steps to complete the phase are discussed. The steps are a combination of tasks to complete, questions to answer, and ideas to consider. We provide examples of the phase in action to illustrate how the framework has been and can be used. We provide tasks for you to complete at the end of each phase. By the end of Part III, you will have an understanding of the framework and how you can use it to facilitate the change process that leads to the adoption of an innovation. This is an important point to internalize—the framework is designed to help change agents go through a process for making change that leads to the adoption of an innovation.

12 | **Phase One: Planning**

Benjamin Franklin quipped, "If you fail to plan, you are planning to fail." This adage unquestionably applies to the change process and innovation adoption. So, it should not come as a surprise that the first phase of the PURPOSE Framework is planning (see Figure 12.1). There are three primary steps to this phase. Step 1 is describing the change that is to be made. Step 2 is determining the goals associated with this change. Step 3 is exploring how others are using the innovation that is part of the change being made. It is important to consider that what we just described are the primary steps. As you will discover when you read more about these steps, there are additional considerations as you go through the three primary steps of the Planning Phase.

 ## Point to Consider: Innovation, Innovation Adoption, Initiative, Intervention, and Change Process

If you read Chapter 4, *Talking the Talk*, you will recall we introduced you to key terms about educational change and innovation adoption. As we begin to discuss the PURPOSE Framework, we will be using many of these terms. In case you need to refresh your meme. So, let's use this as an opportunity to refresh your memory.

Innovation is a noun. It describes a *thing* that is new to you, your school, or your district. An innovation may be curriculum, technology, and instructional practice, or an idea. It can also be two or more of these. For example, an innovation

---

could be a combination of a technology and along with an instructional practice in which the technology is integrated.

Innovation Adoption is a verb. It describes the *action* of purposefully adopting an innovation. It is the intended outcome that results from going through the change process.

Initiative is a noun. An initiative in education is a program that is put into place to address a need or an issue. The initiative includes the innovation, the goals, and context for innovation adoption. An initiative is often the catalyst for engaging in the change process.

Intervention is a verb. An intervention is the combination of the "actions and events that influence the change process" (Hall & Hord, 2020, p. 226).

Change Process is a noun. It describes the *entire series* of events that a change agent facilitates with the end result being the sustained adoption of an innovation.

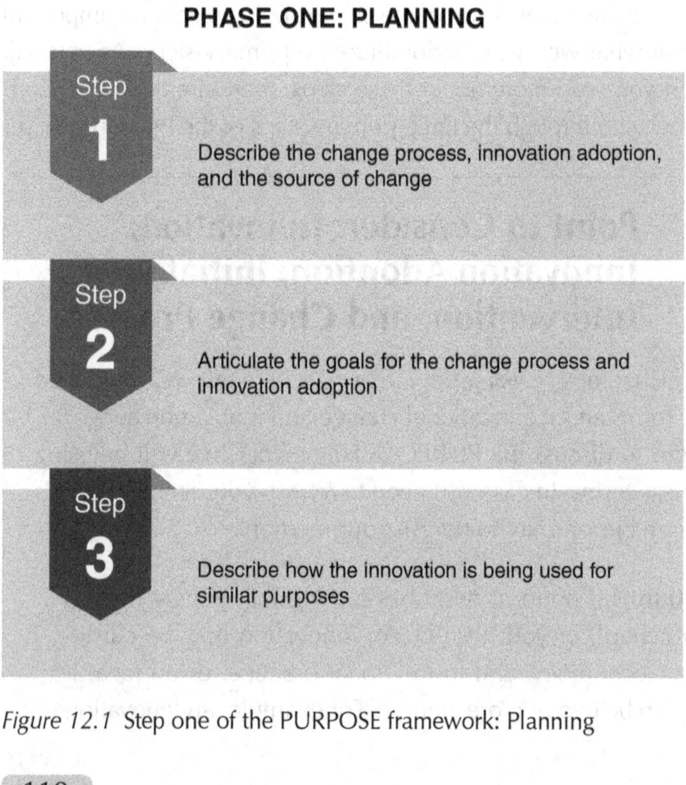

PHASE ONE: PLANNING

Step
1
Describe the change process, innovation adoption, and the source of change

Step
2
Articulate the goals for the change process and innovation adoption

Step
3
Describe how the innovation is being used for similar purposes

Figure 12.1 Step one of the PURPOSE framework: Planning

Steps of the Planning Phase

The primary outcome of the Planning Phase is to clearly describe the change that is being requested. There are multiple elements to this outcome such as understanding who requested the change, who is being asked to change, and why the change was requested. At the end of the Planning Phase, you will have a clear understanding of the change that needs to occur and the innovation that should be adopted. This understanding will help focus your efforts as a change agent responsible for facilitating this change. Figure 12.1 outlines the three steps that you will work through as you complete this phase. It is important to note that there are various questions to answer and tasks to complete as you go through this phase and the remaining phases of the PURPOSE Framework.

 ### Point to Consider: Commitment to the Change Process and the Innovation

Michael Fullan (2007) wrote that, "promoters of change need to be committed to and skilled in the change process as well as the change itself" (p. 108). This is an important idea for you to internalize. What does this mean for us as educational technology change agents? We need to be able to explain clearly what is involved in the change process in addition to having expertise in the change being requested. We *must* be skilled in both. The comforting news is that this is possible. You will gain a strong understanding of the change process by reading this book (and you will have a process to follow—the PURPOSE Framework). Having expertise in the requested change will likely not be difficult, because as an educational technology change agent the requested change (i.e., the innovation to be adopted) you are asked to facilitate will most likely focus on technology.

Steps in Phase One: Planning

Step 1 of the Planning Phase includes **describing the change process, innovation adoption, and the source of change.** To complete this step, you should answer the following questions:

- **How would you describe the change process and innovation adoption?** As a change agent, you will work with individuals who are not familiar with the change process and innovation adoption. It is important that you are able to describe to them what is involved. You should be able to describe the process from a theoretical point-of-view and from a practical perspective. We suggest taking time right now to consider how you would describe what is involved with the change process and innovation adoption if you were presenting an overview at your District Office to a group of stakeholders. We suggest reviewing Part I if you need to refresh your understanding of change theory, the change process, and innovation adoption.

- **Who is the source of the change?** The answer to this question will provide you with insight into the motivation and purpose behind why the change is being requested. Typically, you will be asked by an administrator (most likely a principal, associate superintendent, or superintendent) to be involved in facilitating or leading the change process. It is important to note, however, that a requested change may not have originated from the individual who asked you to be involved in facilitating the change process. Hall and Hord (2020) discussed this notion with the Policy-to-Practice Continuum (p. 16). They indicate that the Policy-to-Practice Continuum often starts at the Federal level and continues down through the state, district, and school levels, and ends with the change being manifested at the school or classroom level. It is important as a change agent to understand where on this continuum the change originated. This will help you understand why the change was requested. Often, the individual who requested that you be involved can provide you with this information.

- **What change is being requested?** It is crucial to have a clear understanding of the requested change. There is little to no chance that the change process and eventual adoption of the innovation will

Point to Consider: A Grassroots Initiation of Change

Although most change is initiated from a top-down approach (policy-to-practice), change can be initiated by an educator or a group of educators. You could be the initiator of change. With this bottom-up approach (practice-to-policy), what often has occurred is dissatisfaction with what is going on in a school or classroom. When considering your involvement as a change agent in a grassroots initiation of change, it is important to realize that the change process and innovation adoption would still occur. It is possible that the process might occur more quickly depending on what the change is. Most likely, the support you provide would be different than if it were top-down initiated change. Finally, it is possible that a change in practice would occur but a change in policy would not.

be successful without this understanding. You need to have a conversation or conversations with the individual who directly requested the change to determine how the individual describes and defines the change. This will help make it clear what is involved with the change you are being asked to facilitate. You will also want to determine what innovation will be adopted. We suggest asking the following questions:

- Is the innovation technology an instructional practice or both?
- What would the innovation look like when implemented?
- Is the innovation intended to be adopted by all at the same time or can it be phased in over time with different groups?
- What is the timeline for innovation adoption?
- What is the catalyst and rationale for the innovation adoption? (Reconfirm this.)
- What problem is the innovation adoption intended to address?
- Why is the innovation needed? Does it align with your why?
- Has consideration been given to how adopting the innovation will impact the learning ecosystem?
- What data are there to support the decision to adopt the innovation?

Point to Consider: The Outcome of the Change Process

As educational technology change agents, often the change we are involved with implementing is the integration of some form of technology into teaching and learning. The technology would be the innovation that would be adopted as a result of going through the change process. We have been involved with assisting several school districts move through the change process. An important idea we have learned is that the result of change can look very different in classrooms located in the same school. In our own research (Donovan, Green, & Hartley, 2010) of a 1:1 laptop program (e.g., the innovation that was adopted) at a middle school, we developed an Innovation Configuration Map (from Concerns-Based Adoption Model [CBAM]) and found that the ways the laptops were being used by students in the classrooms varied greatly. One specific way was no better than another—they were just different. As a change agent, do not be alarmed if you observe an innovation being used in different ways and in ways you may not expect. This will be crucial for you to remember during the last three phases of the PURPOSE Framework.

 Jody's Perspective From the Trenches: Defining the Change Process and the Innovation

My district was in the beginning stages of infusing technology throughout the schools in the district when I moved to the role of teacher on special assignment (TOSA) in educational technology. The local community had recently voted to pass a bond that would fund technology purchases. The district administration at that time was keen on increasing availability of technology in the schools. Although there was a commitment to increased access to technology in the classrooms, there was not a clear shared description of what this would look like when implemented. An Innovation Team was created to develop this description and to determine the outcomes of implementation. The team included the District administrators, Principals, TOSAs, community members, and consultants. We spent months discussing the description and the expected outcomes. The discussions also included conversations about the type of devices to purchase. It took numerous meetings and conversations outside of Innovation Team meetings before clarity was reached. Despite there being a requested change initiated by my District's Superintendent, there was initial uncertainty about important elements about this change. It was difficult to move forward with the change process until this uncertainty was cleared up. It is important to understand that planning for change will be messy. It can take time and it will involve many different people who have competing agendas.

The next step in Planning is to **articulate the goals for the innovation adoption**.

In order to do this, the following should be done:

- You should have an additional conversation with the individual(s) who charged you with leading change process and the innovation adoption. Your goal with this conversation is to come away with a solid understanding of the intended outcomes of adopting this particular innovation. During this conversation, ask the following questions:

  - How much change do you wish to see?
  - What impact are we measuring beyond looking at standardized test scores?
  - How do you define success of this innovation adoption?
  - What are some benchmarks you would be satisfied with?

- You should develop two or three measurable goals. You should do this collaboratively with the individuals who have charged you with leading the innovation adoption. Consider the following as you develop the goals:

  - Improved learner outcomes should be the priority. Include all groups of learners.

- Connect the goals to the source of change you already identified and to school improvement plan goals.

- Include a goal related to teacher professional development.

- Align the evaluation of goals to student learning outcomes, not learning activities.

- Use what you know about writing academic goals. For example, to increase critical thinking skills, all third-grade students will use technology in math at least three times a week.

 ## Point to Consider: Fostering Relationships

Multiple stakeholders will be involved in any change process. The relationships you have with those involved will have a direct effect on the success of the process. Having a poor relationship with a key stakeholder could hinder what you are able to accomplish. This underscores the need for you to be deliberate about fostering relationships. Michal Fullan (2007) emphasized this point, "we have to learn how to develop relationships with those we might not understand and might not like, and vice versa" (p. 115). So, do not underestimate, or take anyone who is part of the change process for granted.

In order to be fully prepared for the understanding phase of the PURPOSE Framework, you will need to be able to **describe how the innovation is being used for similar purposes**. Revisit what you noted regarding goals and intended outcomes for the innovation adoption. Reflect on the conversations you had with the administration regarding what they expect to see when the innovation has been adopted. You can then begin to research ways individuals in your own community may using the innovation and also explore outside your community to discover and connect with those who are using it. You may consider doing any or all of the following:

- Use professional networks such as Twitter, ISTE Professional Learning Networks, local affiliates of your state's technology professional groups, and your state's Department of Education.

- Visit classroom teachers who are using the innovation.
- Search YouTube for videos of people who may be using the innovation.
- If the innovation is a tool, contact the company and ask for introductions to others who are using the innovation.
- Attend a conference.
- Read the professional literature.

 ## Jody's Perspective From the Trenches: Connecting With Like-Minded Colleagues

When I first became a TOSA, I quickly realized that my role was unique and a vast departure from anything my district had experienced before. We had other Academic Coaches in the district who supported district initiatives, but my role was quite different from the other Academic Coaches. Not only was I working with teachers and students to implement mobile devices in the classroom, I was also helping to create district policies regarding technology integration. Although I had support, in many ways I felt like I was all alone in my work. I looked outward for additional support. I became active on Twitter and built my personal learning network to include other technology leaders and coaches. I attended local and international technology conferences and talked to people about leading professional change, and then made social media connections happen with those people in order to remain connected. The number of TOSAs in technology integration grew over the course of a few years in the early part of the 2010s, and there was clearly a need to bring TOSAs together across districts and across the country. #TOSAchat was born in response to the need to share ideas, struggles, and achievements for those of us in the role of an Ed Tech coach. I now have a trusted network of people who are also change agents in their own unique roles, and although many have changed roles, that network is still strong. It is important to remember that you are not the only person who is implementing change in your district or school. Despite your own circumstances and dynamics being unique, we can all learn from one another, support one another, and stay current by sharing how we are working through change and innovation adoption. If you are a coach, TOSA, or even an administrator who is leading change in any way, join in on #TOSAchat or a similar conversation on Twitter. Grow your personal learning network in as many ways as you can. It will help you more than you could ever imagine.

In addition to finding out how others are using the innovation, it is important to reflect on your own use.

- Are you in your current position as a change agent because you were identified as one who is currently using the innovation successfully?
- Are you going to be learning alongside others?
- Perhaps you are a former adopter of the innovation?

How you answer these questions is not important. What is important is that you can discuss in a clearway that allows others to understand your role in supporting the innovation adoption throughout the change process.

To represent yourself as a well-informed change agent, it is important to locate research on the benefits, challenges, and perspectives of the innovation. You can locate research without professional literature subscriptions. Try searching in:

- https://scholar.google.com/
- https://www.merlot.org/merlot/
- https://eric.ed.gov/ (select box for full text available on ERIC)
- https://www.oercommons.org/

A basic Google search of your topic can also lead you to research reports, evaluations, and other published literature on the topic. Many software or hardware companies also publish their own reports (white papers).

After working through the steps in this phase, you should now be in a position to answer questions about the change process and to begin helping others understand the innovation adoption being requested. You should also be aware that things you plan for may change as you move through the change process.

Point to Consider: Funding

Change agents are often involved in grant writing as part of the change process. This is especially true if the change is grassroots initiated. For change to be sustained, there needs to have equal allocation of funds in all three phases (initiation, implementation, institutionalization) of innovation adoption. So, gaining funds needed to support the change process and innovation adoption is critical.

We feel the most difficult part about writing a grant is locating a viable one. There are many resources for grants—educational associations (e.g., NCMA [National Council of Teachers of Mathematics], NEA [National Education Association]), corporations (e.g., Best Buy, Honda, VOYA), foundations (e.g., Gates, Annenburg), and state and Federal agencies.

Once you locate a suitable funding source, you need to ask yourself:

- Do we meet the requirements?
- Is the award feasible given the time it takes to complete the application?
- Does this grant provide funding to support our specific innovation?

We have a few tips to consider as you write a grant application.

- Be passionate, but realistic with what you are proposing.
- Be specific in addressing the prompts on the grant. Use key words or phrases mentioned in the grant purpose and description.
- Always (yes, always!) focus on student learning, not on access to devices or other resources.
- Do not assume the reader has familiarity with your context or the acronyms you use.
- Use a positive voice. Write "I will..." rather than "I hope..."
- Show that you believe all students can learn!

Let's Explore and Practice!

- Create a folder on your computer or purchase a journal to keep track of the notes you take on the different phases of the PURPOSE Framework. We will refer to this in future chapters as your *PURPOSE Journal*.

- Create a presentation that explains the need for innovation adoption as well as an introduction to the innovation.

- Create an infographic or handout that highlights the research supporting the innovation adoption.

- Add your materials from Part II (Contemporary Skills Software chart, Educational Development Framework) to your *PURPOSE Journal*.

- Spend some time looking for grants related to the innovation. Look at the question prompts and begin to write down ideas for how to complete the application. Even if a deadline has passed, most funding agencies have annual application windows when the agency accepts applications.

13 | Phase Two: Understanding

As we have mentioned at different points in the book, change is complex and dynamic. There are numerous elements that we need to attend to if we are to successfully facilitate the change process and bring about innovation adoption. Despite change being complex and dynamic, it can be understood and managed. The primary purpose of the Understanding Phase is to bring about the understanding of elements that directly impact the process so the process can be effectively managed. The understanding is focused on the individuals involved—those who are being asked to changed and adopt the innovation. As such, the primary outcomes of the Understanding Phase will be (1) determining who needs to be involved in the change process and innovation adoption, (2) ensuring that those involved understand the process and what the innovation is, and (3) determining their perceptions of and concerns about the innovation.

As we consider change and innovation adoption, it is important to note that Hall and Hord (2020) indicate that, "organizations adopt change and individuals implement it" (p.18). It is, therefore, highly important that we make every effort to include those who need to be involved in the process (as early and often as possible) and determine their perceptions and concerns about the innovation. Fullan (2016), like Hall and Hord, acknowledges that although the school is typically the unit of change, the individuals (e.g., educators, the principal, the school board) are those that have the most impact on the success of an innovation adoption because they are the ones that must embrace and implement the change.

Steps of the Understanding Phase

There are four main steps that make up this phase. The first step is to make sure you have a clear understanding of the individuals who need to be involved. Second, you will make sure those individuals have an understanding of what you are asking them to do. Hall and Hord (2020), Fullan (2016), and Rogers (2003) suggest that for change to occur and innovation adoption to be sustained, it must be meaningful to the individuals adopting the innovation. The individuals must feel some amount of commitment to the process and to using the innovation if innovation adoption is to be sustained. As a change agent, helping those involved understand what is going on, what their involvement will look like, and what is being requested of them can help bring about commitment to the change process and adopting the innovation.

Third, you need to understand others' perceptions of the innovation. Rogers (2003) discussed this idea as being part of the first phase of innovation adoption—the decision-making phase. Individuals being asked to adopt an innovation will generally ask themselves a series of questions about the innovation. We discussed these in Chapter 5. Being mindful of these questions and the thought process that individuals go through when evaluating an innovation will help you as a change agent to provide the necessary support needed to get individuals committed (and remain committed over time) to the change process and innovation adoption.

Finally, you will need to have a solid understanding of the concerns of the individuals being asked to change and adopt the innovation. Similar to understanding perceptions of the innovation, understanding concerns about innovation adoption is important because it helps the change agent make decisions that will take place during Preparing, Operationalizing, and Sustaining (phases 4, 5, and 6 of the PURPOSE Framework). During the Understanding phase, you will systematically reflect on the types of conversations people are having with you about the change process and innovation adoption. Using the Stages of Concern (SoC) construct of Hall and Hord's (2020) Concerns-based Adoption Model (see Chapter 5), you will gain an understanding of concerns individuals have about the innovation.

Steps to Follow in Understanding

The first step in the Understanding phase is to **identify all individuals that need to be involved in the innovation adoption** (Figure 13.1). Too often we have seen innovation adoption fail because a key group of individuals were not informed or adequately informed about what was to take place, what their involvement would look like, and what was being requested of them. Early on in the change process, it is important that you identify those who need to be involved. We suggest having a conversation with the individual who initiated the change to determine who should be involved. We have included a list of individuals you may need to consider. This list is in

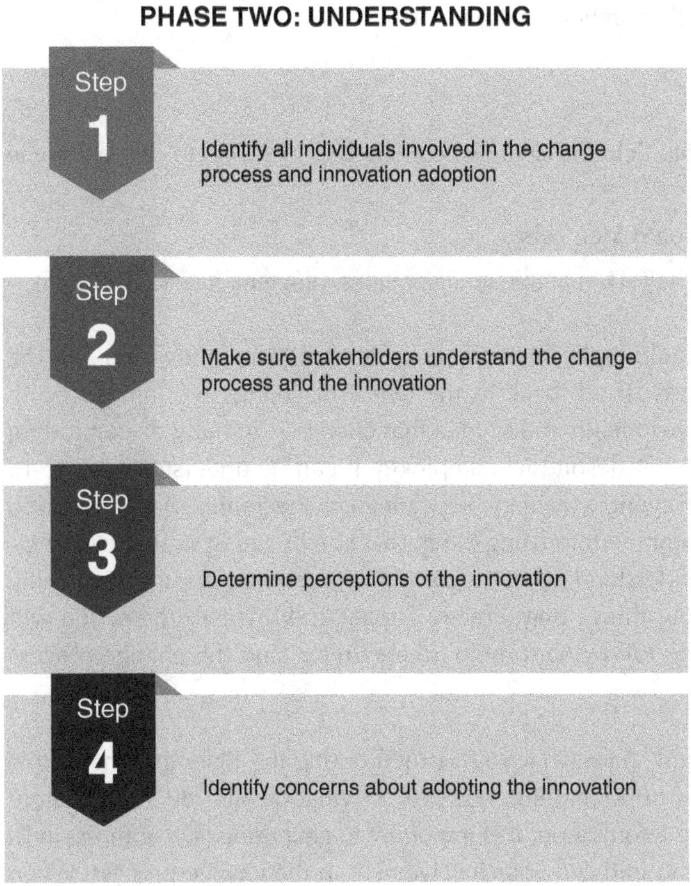

PHASE TWO: UNDERSTANDING

Step 1
Identify all individuals involved in the change process and innovation adoption

Step 2
Make sure stakeholders understand the change process and the innovation

Step 3
Determine perceptions of the innovation

Step 4
Identify concerns about adopting the innovation

Figure 13.1 Step two of the PURPOSE framework: Understanding

alphabetical order rather than in order of importance. Depending on the innovation and the scale of the innovation adoption, when individuals are included would vary. Again, we suggest informing those involved as early as possible.

We suggest considering the following individuals:

- Administration
- Alumni
- Community Members
- Donors
- Educators (including paraprofessionals)
- External Researchers or Evaluators
- Learners
- Parents
- Partnership Schools (schools learners will move on to or have come from)
- School Board Members
- Support Staff (IT, maintenance, facilities, office managers, and staff)

Next, you should **make sure others understand the innovation and the change process**. Think back to the tenets of change we introduced in Chapter 3—specifically to the idea that change is initially discomforting (tenet 2) and that despite its complexity it can be understood (tenet 4). As a change agent, you can help alleviate the initial discomfort and promote commitment to using the innovation by being strategic in helping others understand what is going on. Everyone appreciates being informed about things that directly impact and involves them. You will need to do the following to help others understand the change process and innovation.

- You should share what you learned during the Planning Phase. It is important to be mindful, however, of what details you share. Before you share information, it is important to get permission from the individual who initiated your involvement in the change process. When you have the go-ahead, consider using the materials you may have created from the "Let's Explore ad Practice!" activities at the end of

Chapter 12 (assuming you completed these exercises). Your goal is to help others understand the following:

- What the innovation is (a technology, an instructional practice, or both).
- How the innovation meets the needs of the iMakers.
- A proposed timeline and expectations for adoption process.
- The data used to determine the need for the innovation adoption or the problem being addressed by the innovation adoption.
- What innovation implementation will look like.
- The initial goals for innovation adoption, and how they will be measured.

- If one of your colleagues is already using the innovation, determine how you can capitalize on this. Consider asking your colleague:

  - if other educators can visit their classroom,
  - to discuss the innovation at a staff meeting or during a professional learning community meeting,
  - for a testimonials about how the innovation is working, and
  - to document and share the successes and challenges that have been experienced using the innovation.

- We suggest using a combination of strategies to help others learn more about the change process and the innovation.

  - Classroom visits to those already using the innovation
  - Inviting individuals be part of an innovation adoption committee
  - "Lunch and Learn" sessions to experiment and try the innovation (especially if technology is part of the innovation or it is the innovation)
  - Mandated meetings or orientations
  - Newsletter
  - Parent/Guardian and community information night
  - Personal conversations with those involved
  - Social Media
  - School Board meetings
  - Staff meeting presentation and Q&A
  - Website

As you are making sure individuals have an awareness of the change process and innovation, you should plan on being available for answering questions. We suggest being available synchronously and asynchronously. Once again, use your notes from the Planning Phase. It will be incredibly helpful for completing step 3 if you have taken notes of the questions you've been asked.

Step 3 of the Understanding phase is to **determine individual perceptions of the innovation and perceptions of involvement in its adoption.** Being a careful listener and observer will allow you to accurately gauge the general readiness and willingness that individuals have for adopting the innovation. We introduced the concept of adopter categories in Chapter 4, and in Chapter 5 we introduced Roger's Initiation Phase of innovation adoption. Considering these ideas, we reflect on the individuals involved. In the "Let's Explore and Practice!" section of this chapter, we provided Table 13.1 to help you do this based on Rogers' (2003) characteristics of an innovation. As a reminder, we have included these characteristics in the directly below. We have included questions that as a change agent you might be asked. They are ones we have been asked as change agents.

1. **Relative Advantage:** Is the innovation better than what is in existence? Examples of questions you might be asked.

    a. How is this different from ...?

    b. Why do we need this?

    c. What is so good about it?

    d. Isn't this just a new name for ...?

2. **Compatibility:** Is this innovation consistent with my values, experiences, and needs? Examples of questions you might be asked.

    a. How does this work with our student population?

    b. Does this fit with ... curriculum?

    c. How is this going to help me with ...?

    d. How can I do this in my content area?

    e. Is this going to work with our (LMS, assessment, parent communication, ... and so forth) system?

    f. I don't need more of [the innovation], I need ...!

3. **Complexity:** Is this innovation going to be hard for me to understand and use? Examples of questions you might be asked.

   a. Who is going to teach me how to use it?

   b. What's involved in learning this?

   c. Are you going to train us?

   d. Do the students already know how to use this?

4. **Trialability:** Can I just use this innovation on a trial basis and then decide? Examples of questions you might be asked.

   a. Do we get to try or do we have to use it all the time?

   b. What if I find it's not for me, do I have to continue?

   c. Is everyone going to be using this?

5. **Observability:** Will others be able to tell that things have changed? Examples of questions you might be asked.

   a. What is this going to look like?

   b. How will this show in test scores?

   c. How will parents know what's going on?

Understanding the reactions individuals have to being asked to adopt an innovation will help you gauge perceptions about innovation adoption, and to a lesser extent the innovation itself. Both Rogers (2003) and Fullan (2016) stress the importance of this during the initiation phase of innovation adoption. You will be using what you learn about people's perceptions (both good and bad) of the innovation during the Researching Phase of the PURPOSE Framework.

Providing individuals with opportunities to talk about the innovation is one of the best approaches to understanding their perceptions about the change process and innovation. It will not be difficult to get a sense of how individuals perceive the innovation. You will most likely be able to tell by gestures and facial expressions. You should also pay attention to the questions they ask and their overall level of interest. We suggest you group the individuals you will be working with during the innovation adoption into three groups based on how you have gauged their perceptions of the innovation. We discuss these groups based on Rogers' Adopter Categories (see Chapter 4) despite the individuals at this point in the change process not actually having adopted the innovation yet.

1. **Ready to go!** These individuals have a positive perception of both the change process and the innovation. According to Rogers (2003), these individuals would be the Innovators and Early Majority. They may be considered "tech-savvy" but not necessarily. These individuals are those who are open to trying something new even if they do not know much about it. They are those who were less concerned about the *compatibility* and *complexity* of the innovation. They may or may not need your support in understanding and implementing the innovation. These people showed excitement and were not intimidated by the innovation.

2. **Still deciding.** These individuals have a somewhat neutral perception of the innovation. These are the individuals who need more information. They probably had many questions about the *observability* of the innovation as well as about its *complexity*. They would be considered the Late Majority based on Rogers's (2003) Adopter Categories. These individuals will need support throughout the entire innovation adoption.

3. **Not so much!** These individuals are either not happy about being asked to try something new, or they may not have a very favorable perception of the innovation. These are—as you know doubt guessed—the Laggards. These individuals are not motivated to implement the innovation for a range of reasons. You can gain an understanding of these reasons by reflection on the questions they asked you. Negative perceptions about the innovation would be represented by many questions about *relative advantage*. Not being happy about being asked to try something new could stem from lack of confidence (represented by questions about *complexity*) or a lack of understanding of the innovation (represented by questions about *complexity* and *observability*). Others may not be happy about being asked to change as they are skeptical about what seems to be a never-ending cycle of "new things." These individuals will not only ask you many questions about *relative advantage*, they will share with you their experiences with previous innovation adoptions.

The final step in the Understanding Phase is to consider perceptions of the innovation in context—that is, you will need to **identify the concerns regarding innovation adoption**. Think about Fullan (2016) and the multiple dimensions in the meaning of educational change (see Chapter 5). We know that educational environments are dynamic ecosystems with

Table 13.1 Stages of Concern from Hall and Hord (2020): Descriptions, Elements to Observe, and Questions to Ask

Stage	Description	Things to Listen for
Unconcerned	Just beginning to think about the innovation but not concerned about it at all	• I've got other things going on right now. • I'm not even sure what you are talking about. • I don't really care about ….
Informational	Interested but not concerned beyond curiosity	• What resources are available to help us? • How is this better than what we have now? • I need to hear more about it.
Personal	Concerned about own role ·	• Who will be making the decisions? • How is this going to affect me? • How much time and energy do I need to invest?
Management	Concerned about how to use the innovation	• I'm really busy (being grade-level chair), I don't have a lot of time. • I'm not sure I can do all this on top of what I already do. • How is this going to work in the [Art/PE] classroom?
Consequence	Concerned about how innovation is impacting others	• Do we know what the students think about it? • How can we get students excited about this? • I think students need to be involved.
Collaboration	Concerned about how best to share with others	• Let me know if you want me to talk to others. • (XYZ) is already doing something like this—let's talk to them • I think I want to collaborate with ….
Refocusing	Concerned about modifying or replacing the innovation	• I've been doing this already, I'm thinking of … • How can we add to this? • I think this would work better if we …

multiple elements. We also know that individuals in the ecosystem have circumstances that affect them that are not part of the educational eco-system. As change agents, we need to have an understanding of the big picture so we can determine how best to support those being asked to implement the innovation.

We introduced you to Hall and Hord's (2020) SoC in Chapter 5. We are huge advocates of this process and use it in our own research. Hall and Hord (2020) developed the Stages of Concern Questionnaire (SoCQ) as a tool to determine concerns. Fortunately, the SoCQ is easily available on the Internet. Unfortunately, analyzing the response data is a very com-plex process that requires training. Despite this, you can still get a sense of concerns by being a good listener and observer and by asking pointed questions.

Hall and Hord (2020) identified seven SoC. We represent these in Table 13.1 with some potential phrases you might associate with each stage.

Asking pointed questions will help you gain a general sense of con-cerns related to being asked to adopt the innovation. You will have general sense of how people are feeling about being asked to try something new. Using this information and the potential adopter groups you identified, you should be well prepared to move on to Researching. We want to be clear, however, that asking questions and being a good listener and observer will not give you as complete a picture of concerns as you would gain if you were to complete an SoCQ, analyze the data, and develop SoC profiles.

 ## Jody's Perspective From the Trenches: Understanding

When we began our implementation of 1:1 mobile devices, we conducted a SoCQ with our teachers and administrators. It was interesting to see that we had teachers who fell into each of the seven categories. Using this data, we were able to focus in on some of the concerns that could become potential barriers to implemen-tation. We added teacher's concerns to their school's Technology Plan, and we discussed ways in which to best support teachers based on their stage of concern through school- and district-based professional learning.

Let's Explore and Practice!

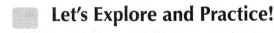

- Visit the classroom of an individual who has already adopted the innovation and take photos or make a short movie. Add this information to your PURPOSE Journal that you began in Phase One: Planning.

- Speak to your administrator and arrange to be on the schedule for staff meetings and/or school events to introduce stakeholders to the innovation.

- Revisit the infographic/handout you created at the end of the Planning Phase. Disseminate it to parents and community members.

- Create a chart that aligns the use of the innovation to the learning preferences of the iMakers (from Part II). Add this to your PURPOSE Journal.

- Send a one-item survey to determine current stages of adoption. Ask teachers to select the statement that best represents their current feeling toward (the innovation)].

  - Being asked to do this makes me nervous
  - I'm willing to try integrating (the innovation)
  - I'm getting better at using (the innovation)
  - I'm confident in using (the innovation)
  - I'm so good at using (the innovation), I could teach others

- Create and share a survey with teachers, staff, and administration that is based on the SoCQ. You can also use these questions in general conversations with the individuals you are supporting during innovation adoption. For example:

  - What is your familiarity with (the innovation)?
  - What is your experience with (the innovation)?
  - Do you feel students would benefit from (the innovation)?
  - Do you feel you will benefit from (the innovation)?
  - What do you see as strengths of (the innovation)?
  - What do you see as issues with (the innovation)?
  - Are you ready to adopt (the innovation)?

- Add Table 13.2 or create a page for columns two and three of the table to your PURPOSE Journal. You will notice we did not include a section for those who are ready to go. You may choose to add this column. Spend time reflecting on how to complete the second row.

Table 13.2 Examples of Questions to Ask and the People Who Ask These Questions During the Understanding Phase

Category	Still Deciding	Not so much
Examples of questions	• Can I just use this innovation on a trial basis and then decide? • Do we get to try or do we have to use it all the time? • What if I find it's not for me, do I have to continue? • Is everyone going to be using this? • What is this going to look like? • How will this show in test scores? • How will parents know what's going on? • Who is going to teach me how to use it? • What's involved in learning this? • Are you going to train us? • Do the students already know how to use this?	• How is this different from …? • Why do we need this? • What is so good about it? • Isn't this just a new name for …? • Does this fit with … curriculum? • How is this going to help me with …? • How can I do this in my content area? • Is this going to work with our (LMS, assessment, parent communication, …) system? • I don't need more of (the innovation), I need …!
People asking these questions		

Phase Three: Researching

The Researching Phase of the PURPOSE Framework allows you to apply what you gained from the Understanding Phase and will help you with the Preparing Phase (Phase Four). Fullan (2016) suggests that the initiation phase of innovation adoption is where decisions are being made and plans are being established about how to assist individuals in adopting an innovation. We consider the Planning, Understanding, and Researching phases to be similar to what Fullan calls the initiation phase of change because you are gathering information and making decisions about innovation adoption during these phase. So far with phases one and two, you have spent time planning for and understanding the innovation, the intended innovation adoption, and the individuals involved. You now move on to Researching—the third phase in the PURPOSE Framework.

Steps of the Researching Phase

This phase has two steps. The first step is identifying Intervention Mushrooms (Hall & Hord, 2020) and Opinion Leaders (Rogers, 2003). We discussed these groups of individuals in Chapters 4 and 5. In step 2, you will revisit what you learned about Hall and Hord's (2020) CBAM (Concerns-Based Adoption Model) Stages of Concern and use this understanding to identify sources of concerns regarding innovation adoption. Having knowledge of key individuals and sources of concerns will assist you in making informed decisions during the Preparing Phase—the next phase of the PURPOSE Framework.

Point to Consider: The Role of Interventions in the Change Process

It is important as a change agent to be aware of the role of interventions during the change process. As noted in a previous Point to Consider, interventions are the actions or events that influence innovation adoption (Hall & Hord, 2020). Interventions can occur during any time of the change process. Interventions can be intentional (e.g., a planned meeting) or accidental (e.g., delayed delivery of the innovation). Hall and Hord use the terms sponsored and unsponsored. Sponsored or unsponsored, these events and subsequent actions can play a pivotal role in the success of innovation adoption. As change agents, we can plan ahead for potential unsponsored interventions by being well prepared.

 ## Steps to Follow in the Researching Phase

The Researching Phase begins with **identifying key individuals** (Figure 14.1). You will do this by reflecting on what you learned about your colleagues during the Understanding Phase. Refer back to the notes you took if you completed the "Let's Explore and Practice" exercises at the end of the

PHASE THREE: RESEARCHING

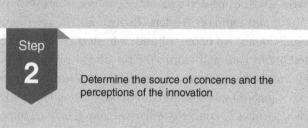

Step 1 — Identify key individuals

Step 2 — Determine the source of concerns and the perceptions of the innovation

Figure 14.1 Step three of the PURPOSE framework: Researching

Understanding Phase. In an attempt to understand your colleagues' readiness, we suggested you try to understand their perception of the innovation as well as their concerns regarding adopting the innovation. As you considered perceptions, we suggested you looked through the lens of Rogers' (2003) Adopter Categories at those being asked to change. The purpose was to loosely identify three groups of people: those "ready to go," those "still deciding," and those "not-so-much" ready to go (see Chapter 13). When considering concerns, although you did not complete a formal SoCQ (Stages of Concern Questionnaire), you used Hall and Hord's (2020) Stages of Concern definitions to determine and understand what individuals were concerned about regarding their involvement in the innovation adoption.

There are two groups of individuals to look out for as you identify key individuals. The first group is the *Opinion Leaders* (Rogers, 2003) or the *Intervention Mushrooms* (Hall & Hord, 2020). Opinion Leaders can be positive or negative; Intervention Mushrooms can be Nutritious or Poisonous. Rogers (2003) suggests that Opinion Leaders are informal leaders whose behavior is considered by others to be in line with the norm for the group (p. 27). More often than not, the Opinion Leaders will positively impact the innovation adoption process. To this extent, Opinion Leaders are the individuals who people can relate, who are respected by their peers, and who are often given a platform to communicate their opinions and ideas. The Opinion Leaders are generally part of Early Majority Adopter Category. They are the people who are willing to try something new but are not necessarily the first to try it.

Similar to identifying positive Opinion Leaders, Hall and Hord (2020) suggest that we need to be aware of Nutritious Mushrooms. These are the individuals who can have a positive influence because their enthusiasm is contagious. Hall and Hord suggest Nutritious Mushrooms are often the individuals with Impact Concerns (p. 237). They are the people who ask about the consequences that innovation adoption can have on student learning. They are excited to collaborate with others on adopting and even modifying the innovation. They often focus some of their energy into sharing the "strengths and successes they are experiencing in using the innovation" (p. 237). These individuals are easy to identify.

The second type of individual you want to keep make sure you area aware of what Hall and Hord refer to as Poisonous Mushrooms (they are similar to Opinion Leaders who negatively impact the innovation adoption process). According to Hall and Hord (2020, p. 235), these are the individuals who have increased personal concerns about the innovation adoption. Hall and Hord indicate that one Poisonous Mushroom can quickly lead to a cluster of Poisonous Mushrooms. Poisonous Mushroom are easily identified because they are extremely vocal in expressing personal concerns and seek the validation others about these negative perception of the innovation or innovation adoption process. Negative Opinion Leaders express similar sentiments. It is important to be diligent in completing step 2 of the Researching Phase if you are to mitigate the issues negative Opinion Leaders and Poisonous Mushrooms can cause.

The next step in the Researching Phase is to **determine the source of concerns and perceptions of the innovation** that individuals (especially Opinion Leaders and Poisonous Mushrooms) have expressed. You should complete the following tasks:

- **Revisit What You Did During the Planning Phase.** If you completed the exercises at the end of Chapter 12, check your notes determine if you did not provide enough information about the innovation and the innovation adoption process. You should revise and reshare if you feel you did not. You may be able to alleviate concerns by sharing or resharing information that may have been missed during the Planning.

- **Spend Time With Individuals.** Talk with them and let them talk with you about what is going on regarding the innovation adoption and other obligations they have. We all have the desire to be heard. Letting individuals talk with you could be the opportunity they need to work through concerns they have.

- **Revisit What You Learned During the Understanding Phase Regarding Concerns.** Some concerns are not related to the innovation but rather they are an indication that the innovation adoption is coming at a time when individuals are overwhelmed or otherwise not ready to embrace change. Knowing this can help you address concerns that may hinder change taking place.

We suggest that you revisit the steps in this phase multiple times during the change process and innovation adoption. Concerns can change.

Perceptions can as well. Having a good handle on the concerns and perceptions throughout the change process will help you successfully facilitate innovation adoption. The more information you have—the more targeted your support can be.

 ## Jody's Perspective From the Trenches: Understanding

Choosing which teachers would initially be participating in the implementation of 1:1 device initiative was primarily determined by the administration. A decision was made that the implementation would happen at specific grade levels for the first deployment of devices. Within each of those grade levels, two teachers from each school were chosen to be the first to receive their devices. In some cases, those teachers were volunteers, and in other cases, they were "voluntold." I was fortunate that at most grade levels the participating teachers were either innovators or Early Adopters, but in some cases I dealt with teachers who were not as ready for this type of change. I made it a point to use the data from our SoCQ, in addition to the data I had personally collected regarding those who were in potential adopter category groups, as I planned for and supported implemented in the first phase. More than anything, after the first wave of teachers were trained, I was able to identify where to spend most of my time. I knew which teachers were ready to move forward with implementation and which teachers were not quite ready. As you identify your adopter groups, know that you will make the most impact somewhere in the middle. The teachers who are already off and running with the innovation or those who adopt quickly are going to make that change regardless of whether you are involved or not. Those who have intense concerns and are not interested in the innovation at all will not be easily swayed. Your time is best spent with those who are in the middle; those who might need some extra support but are willing and excited to change. Focus your time and energy there, and that gentle breeze will start up. Before you know it, you will be working with those who were resistant at first.

Point to Consider: Working With Intervention Mushrooms

Hall and Hord (2020, p. 231) suggest that Intervention Mushrooms are a result of how an individual has interpreted the innovation or their role in innovation adoption. If we can intervene, we can prevent the negativity of the Poisonous Mushroom from spreading. Left unchecked, two or more negative individuals can quickly become a large group of negative individuals. When working with Poisonous Mushrooms, Hall and Hord suggest we are aware of the fact that their insecurity can lead to overreaction to and misinterpretation of ideas being presented. When considering that Poisonous Mushrooms often develop out of concerns related to self (e.g., insecurity, fear of incompetence), it is crucial that change agents take time to listen to their concerns and assure the individual that we are there to support them. Avoid pacifying them with "trust me, this is different" comments (Hall & Hord, 2020, p. 237), as these is often misinterpreted by the individuals that their concerns are not being understood. We also need to make sure we pay attention to Nutritious Mushrooms. In stark contrast to Poisonous Mushrooms and not wanting their numbers to increase, we want our Nutritious Mushrooms to flourish and their numbers to increase. We need to give these individuals opportunities to share, and we need to support them in their collaborations and redefinitions of the innovation adoption.

 # Research to Consider: Concerns About Innovation Adoption

In Chapter 4, we discussed research we have conducted on how we have used the CBAM Stages of Concern to examine innovation adoption. We are not the only ones who have conducted research using the Stages of Concern to make informed decisions about education. We've include three citations to research that has focused on the application of Stages of Concern in teaching and learning. These articles provide excellent perspectives on how understanding and dealing with concerns can help improve teaching and learning.

Bullard, M. B., Rutlidge, C. B., & Koehler-Evans, P. (2017). Using the stages of concern questionnaire to ensure professional development for teachers and teacher candidates. *International Journal of Research in Higher Education*, *2*(4), 50–57.

Charalambous, C., & Philippou, G. (2010). Teachers' concerns and efficacy beliefs about implementing a mathematics curriculum reform: Integrating two lines of inquiry. *Educational Studies in Mathematics*, *75*, 1–21.

Senin, S., & Nasri, N. M. (2019). Teachers' concern towards applying computational thinking skills in teaching and learning. *International Journal of Academic Research in Business and Social Sciences*, *9*(1), 296–310.

Let's Explore and Practice!

- Interview an individual who has already adopted the innovation. Focus your interview on challenges and how they were overcome. Also, seek information on tips and tricks for successful use. Add what you learn to your PURPOSE Journal.

- Revisit the exercises from the Planning Phase (Chapter 12). We suggest that you specifically refresh your memory on any research on the innovation and similar innovation adoptions.

- Revisit the exercises from the Understanding Phase, particularly the SoCQ and the Adopter Category table that we suggested you completed in the "Let's Explore and Practice!" section at the end of Chapter 13.

15 | Phase Four: Preparing

The Preparing Phase is similar to the final phase of what Fullan (2016) calls the Initiation Phase of change and innovation adoption. The primary outcome of the Preparing Phase is to ensure that everyone involved is adequately ready (well, prepared) to begin the next phase—Operationalizing. The Operationalizing Phase primarily focuses on the innovation being adopted by individuals into their practice in different ways and not necessarily at the same rate (more about this in Chapter 16).

As a reminder, when we gave an overview of the PURPOSE Framework in Chapter 11, we visually portrayed the framework as a linear process. Additionally, as we have been describing the phases, we have been going through each phase as if framework is a linear process. Despite this portrayal, the framework is most effective as a recursive process. When using the framework to facilitate change and innovation adoption, you will likely revisit the Planning, Understanding, and Researching Phases multiple times before moving on to the Preparing Phase. You will definitely use the information gathered during these phases as you work through this phase. If you feel you need additional information, we encourage you to revisit the previous phases to gather the information needed.

Steps of the Preparing Phase

There are three steps to the Preparing Phase. You will, as we mentioned, use much of the information and insights gained from the first three phases of the PURPOSE Framework during this phase. First, you will revisit the list of stakeholders who are involved in the innovation adoption process to determine their needs associated with the implementing the innovation. This will help assure that individuals will be prepared for Phase 4: Operationalizing. The second step involves a shift in your role. Up to now you have been involved in foundational work that has placed you in the role of a top-down change agent. You have been mostly concerned with macro-level elements of the innovation adoption process. Your role now starts to shift to that of the bottom-up change agent role. You will be involved in more micro-level elements as you spend increased amounts of time with those who are asked to adopt the innovation. The final step in the Preparing Phase is pivotal to the success of the innovation adoption, and is a step that requires you to invest a great deal of time and energy. This step involves planning, implementing, and evaluating professional development (PD) to support those who are asked to adopt the innovation.

 ## Steps to Follow in the Preparing Phase

The first step in the Preparing Phase is to **determine the needs of those involved in the innovation adoption** (Figure 15.1). You should revisit the list of those who are involved in the innovation adoption. The first need to determine is the equipment resources needed to adopt the innovation. We suggest using a table similar to Table 15.1. If you are keeping a *PURPOSE Journal*, we suggest that you add this table or one like it to your journal. You can add rows for different stakeholders or groups of stakeholders.

 ## Equipment Needs

We acknowledge that determining equipment resource needs may be beyond the scope of your professional responsibilities. We do believe, however, that as a change agent you are in a position to advocate for the necessary equipment resources (actually, all resources) that educators should have to adopt the innovation. Consider what the innovation is that is being adopted and use your expertise to determine all of the necessary equipment. We should not assume that someone else will have done this.

The next set of needs to consider the professional learning needs of those involved. It can be difficult to be specific about all of the professional learning that is needed. However, by considering the information gathered during earlier phases of the PURPOSE Framework, you will be in a good

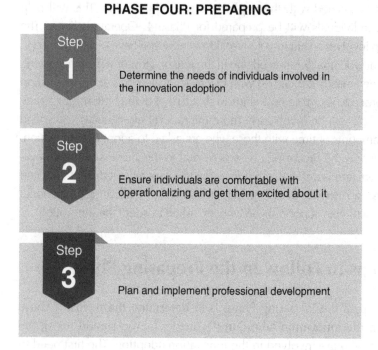

PHASE FOUR: PREPARING

Step 1
Determine the needs of individuals involved in the innovation adoption

Step 2
Ensure individuals are comfortable with operationalizing and get them excited about it

Step 3
Plan and implement professional development

Figure 15.1 Step four of the PURPOSE framework: Preparing

Table 15.1 Determining Who Needs to Be Involved

Stakeholder	Equipment Needed	Person Responsible	Timeline
Add who they are in this column.	List all equipment (e.g., hardware, software, storage, accounts,) needed by the individual in the learning environment. Make sure you consider the home environment as well.		It is okay to be general. For example, IT will need to have everything they need as soon as possible. Educators, however, should be provided with any technology or materials as soon as possible. Our experience and research suggests that educators should be provided with devices for personal use well in advance of when they are expected to use the devices for professional use.

position to develop an overall plan for PD. We recommend you start broad and work your way toward a more detailed PD plan. We recommend you:

- Refresh your understanding on the integration models (SAMR [Substitution, Augmentation, Modification, Redefinition], TPACK [Technological, Pedagogical, and Content Knowledge], TIM [Technology Integration Matrix], see Chapter 9) we discussed in Part II.

- Refresh your memory on the innovation adoption goals gathered during Phase One: Preparing (Chapter 12).

- Review the list of questions (and who asked them) about the innovation and the innovation adoption process (Chapter 13). This list can be used to guide professional learning that is needed. It can be used to identify who needs what type of professional learning.

- Review your stages of adoption one-item survey results gathered during Phase Two: Understanding (Chapter 13).

- Reflect on who you identified as Opinion Leaders, Nutritious Mushrooms, and Poisonous Mushrooms during Phase Three: Researching (Chapter 14).

- Revisit the concerns survey results from Phase Two: Understanding (Chapter 13).

Based on this information, you will be able to organize individuals into groups according to their current perception of the innovation, concerns regarding the innovation adoption, and their current level of proficiency and comfort with the innovation. We suggest organizing this information in Table 15.2.

Table 15.2 Example of How to Determine Professional Development Needs

Stakeholder (Individual or Group)	Professional Learning Needed	Potential Support or Support Lead	Timeline
This is an example	• Introductory • Basic use • General issues (e.g., classroom management, privacy, and safety) • Advanced • Individual needs	Nutritious mushrooms Opinion leaders Early adopters	This is the most difficult aspect to complete; we recommend that you simply consider before implementation, during implementation, or on-going as you consider the timeline for when the professional learning should occur

Professional Learning Needs

You will use the data from Table 15.2 in your next step in Preparing for Operationalizing—that is, **ensuring others are comfortable with and excited about operationalizing**. There are several tasks you can do to get people comfortable with and to generate excitement about the upcoming operationalizing (Phase 5). We provide two lists of suggestions in the next two paragraphs. These suggestions are not listed in any particular order and should not be one-time events. These are suggestions that should be consistently considered (and used!).

First, you will need to spend time addressing questions and concerns to help Laggards and Poisonous Mushrooms be more comfortable with the innovation and the innovation adoption process. We suggest you take time on a regular basis to have one-on-one conversations with them. Please keep in mind, however, that you can easily get trapped into spending a great deal of time with Laggards and Poisonous Mushrooms. Although we want everyone to adopt the innovation, we need to be realistic. It can be extremely difficult to get everyone to adopt an innovation. Your time is precious. Use it wisely and where you can help individual the most who are willing to change. Finally, you know your colleagues best; consider their unique concerns or perceptions as well as their ongoing and ever changing needs as you choose how best to support them. We suggest the following (for all individuals, not just Laggards and Poisonous Mushrooms):

- Be an active listener.
- Cover their class so they can observe the innovation being used in another classroom.
- Plan with them. Co-teach with them. Conduct a demonstration lesson.
- Let them know that they are not alone and that individuals adopt an innovation at different rates.
- Remind and reassure them you are there to support.
- Share the research you gathered during the Planning Phase about the benefits of the innovation. Focus on student learning outcomes.

Second, you will need to build excitement within the whole group including the administration for operationalizing. Again, use what you know about your colleagues and what will work best. We have a few suggestions.

- Have "playground time" (depending on the innovation). For example, if you have a new Maker Space invite everyone in to play in the space. You could hold a meeting in the space and make sure individuals can get a sense of how the space can be used.
- Be procedural at meetings about how you talk about the innovation. Discuss what is going on with the innovation adoption process. Share how individuals are adopting the innovation. Share successes. Share how challenges have been overcome (or being dealt with).
- Generate excitement by using games and healthy competition related to the adoption of the innovation. Award small prizes (who doesn't enjoy food or a beverage?).
- If possible, take a field trip to see the innovation in action.
- Always focus on the benefit of enhance learning.

The next step in the Preparing Phase is to **plan and implement PD.** At this point, you will have a solid understanding of the overall professional learning needs to focus on for PD. You should have a sense of the concerns

Point to Consider: Establishing a Mentoring Relationship

When we think of PD, often we only consider the PD we have received. Take a minute and think about someone who has helped you learn a new skill or process over a period of time. This mentoring PD relationship is as important or possibly more important than the traditional whole-group sessions you have attended. We are sure you can identify potential mentees. Consider some of the Poisonous Mushrooms or Laggards you have identified. You should approach your role as a mentor in the same way you would plan PD. Together with the mentee develop goals, have set times you meet, have specific topics to address, and complete tasks in between. Keep in mind that your job is to support their professional growth—it is not to do their work.

individuals have, which can help you plan appropriate and differentiated PD. In addition, as a result of knowledge you gained during the Researching Phase, you should have solid understanding of best practices and benefits of the innovation being adopted. This can be a focus of PD. Finally, Chapter 9 included a list of software aligned to the contemporary skills (Figure 9.4)—these could be the focus of professional learning related to the innovation. Keep all these sources of information in mind as you develop your PD plan.

 Point to Consider: One-Shot and One-Size Professional Development

We know that for PD to be successful, it cannot be a one-time event or a one-size-fits-all event. The research is clear about this. We have all attended a one-size-fits-all district or school-level PD and left feeling frustrated that we did not gain anything. We have also attended one-shot PD only to leave feeling frustrated with not knowing how to actually apply what we learned to our own learning environment. These memories should be a reminder that there must be ongoing PD and follow-up support to ensure that professional learning actually happens.

Planning Professional Development

The PD plan will be implemented prior to the Operationalizing Phase. However, professional learning should continue throughout the innovation adoption process. Professional learning is integral to Operationalizing and Sustaining the innovation adoption. As such, we strongly encourage you to take the time needed to develop a PD plan that provides for on-going professional learning opportunities.

As with instructional planning, planning PD should be aligned to standards and have clearly stated goals. You can use a chart like Table 15.3 to draft your standards, goals, and evaluation. We have provided an example that outlines professional learning focusing on increasing critical thinking skills of learners through the use of iPads.

Table 15.3 Example of How to Outline Professional Development Learning Goals

Innovation adoption Goal (from Planning with Administration)	ISTE Standards for Educators and/or ISTE Standards for Students	Professional Development Goal	Evaluation Innovation Adoption Goal PD Goal
		Example	
Learners will use iPads to increase critical thinking skills. (This is based on schoolwide data showing that students are not able to apply critical thinking skills across the curriculum at all grade levels.)	ISTE-E 3b ISTE-E 5b ISTE-E 6a, b, c, d ISTE-S 3b, c, d ISTE-S 4a, b, c, d	Teachers will have at least three PD sessions focused on student use of technology for critical thinking. Teachers who request mentoring will have on-going mentoring for at least 1 year.	**Innovation Adoption Goal** Lesson plan analysis, classroom visits **PD Goal** School calendar, PD attendance sign ins

Once you have clearly articulated goals for PD, you should develop an academic year PD calendar. One of the most difficult tasks in planning PD is finding time that works for everyone who needs to attend. As you develop your academic year PD calendar, we a few suggests that you should consider.

- Starting the PD over the summer if possible.
- Having some whole group sessions as well as some small group (required and optional) sessions.
- Include and online/virtual sessions.
- Being consistent with the day and time for the sessions. For example, if your school has PLC time, ask the administrator if one day a month can be dedicated to formal PD. This could be broken down by grade level or content area groups.

In the Researching Phase, you identified individuals who may need more personal PD in the form of mentoring. Mentoring is discussed in a previous Point to Consider. A third form of PD we suggest considering is online professional learning.

Jody's Perspective From the Trenches: The Role of Online Professional Development Modules in Preparing

The implementation of our mobile devices began toward the end of a school year. We wanted teachers to be able to plan over the summer and make use of their new knowledge as they started putting together lessons for the following school year. We also wanted teachers to learn about using a learning management system in the classroom. So, we decided to offer our three PD courses online, as well as, offering the courses in person. We conducted a survey prior to beginning the courses. Teachers were interested in attending PD sessions online. However, our implementation of online PD was different than what you might find in a university or elsewhere; rather than attend an in-person PD session with me, teachers were to choose dates that worked best for them and then attend the PD online instead. They were still required to be on campus and write sub-plans for a guest teacher; however, they just did so on a date that worked best for them rather than the dates I provided for the face-to-face sessions. We experienced a number of challenges throughout the process, and most of the teachers who attended the PD online regretted it and wished they had attended in person. That was not exactly the reaction we were hoping for. We have a wide range of comfort with technology integration in our district, and there are definitely some teachers who want to be in the room with the "expert" in order to have their questions answered quickly and efficiently. Despite the initial challenges we had with online PD, more of our teachers have been attending online PD and webinars, which is an indication that more may be ready to engage in professional learning opportunities offered online. If you are in a similar situation where you want to offer the PD online but you are worried that no one will use it, rest assured that you are not alone! I suggest create the online PD for those who are willing and ready to take advantage of the opportunity. Over time, more teachers will take advantage of these opportunities as they hear about from others.

Point to Consider: Online Professional Development

With teachers being busy and schools not providing less time for attending PD, many educators are opting for online PD. Online PD can come in different forms such as participating in MOOC (Massive Online Open Course), viewing webinars, completing online modules created by professional organizations or content specialists, and completing tutorials on LinkedIn Learning. Although these forms of online PD are viable for many, as a change agent, you can create online PD modules that are very specific to your innovation and innovation adopters. For example, using the school Learning Management System or creating a classroom in Google Classroom, you could create an introductory module that helps the user learn the basics of a new tool and will prepare them for a small group PD session on how to actually integrate the tool for enhancing student learning.

When creating an online module, you will apply the same best practices you do in planning a learning experience for learners.

- Introduce yourself, the topic, and participation expectations. Include an overview/look forward of the module and how the participant should proceed.
- Share a range of resources (videos, step-by-step directions, examples, websites, related literature).
- Provide opportunities for authentic interaction between participants. For example, share a draft of something created and give/receive peer feedback.
- Be an active participant.
- Provide an opportunity for participant feedback so you can improve the module in the future.
- Use Universal Design for Learning principles to guide your development of the module.

We recommend at least one form of PD each month. You might start the year with a whole-group session for a significant amount of time (perhaps a half-day). In subsequent months, offer smaller-sized sessions (for less time) or online sessions based on what you continue to see as professional learning needs. Make sure to get others involved in providing PD. Revisit your lists of Opinion Leaders and Nutritious Mushrooms to find individuals who could be involved in providing PD.

 Point to Consider: Differentiated Professional Development

In order to maximize time and space, many schools have a dedicated PD day held on site. Despite what you may have experienced, it is possible to have a whole school PD day that includes differentiation. To start the day, begin with a whole-group session. Use the whole-group session to provide a theoretical foundation on the topic. Think about connecting the innovation to SAMR (see Chapter 9), providing research on best practice, and showing video vignettes of the innovation in practice. Next, allow individuals to select a breakout session to attend. The breakout sessions can be led by your Opinion Leaders and Nutritious Mushrooms. These sessions could be organized based on proficiency or comfort. The sessions could focus on a specific topic such as classroom management, assessment, and integration strategies.

In addition to a timeline of potential PD, you must also have a method for evaluating the impact of the PD on meeting the initiative goals, as well as the long-term PD goals. Deciding on evaluation of technology plan goals and PD goals is not dissimilar to what you do as an educator when completing long-term planning or evaluating classroom goals and objectives.

Professional Development Session Preplanning

This section is intended to guide you in planning a small-group PD session. If you have not conducted PD with colleagues, you will probably feel quite nervous. We suggest consider the following:

- Is your session an introduction or a continuation of a topic?
- Who are your attendees? Keep in mind what you learned during the Understanding Phase. It is highly important to know as much as you can about those who will be attending.

- Decide on a foundation for your session. Is it going to be meeting the needs of iMakers? SAMR? Universal Design for Learning? A specific contemporary skill such as collaboration or critical thinking? Doing this will shift the focus of your session away from learning a tool to using technology to address the school goals. Make sure this is a clear extension of your innovation adoption goals and your PD goals.

- Spend time locating at least one resource on your topic. Think about a video, a snippet from a TED Talk, a cartoon, an image, an inspirational video or quote, or an activity. You can use this to begin a conversation and get people interested in your topic at the start of the session.

- Are attendees going to need access to specific technology?

- How are you going to share content with attendees? We always recommend going paperless and modeling effective use of technology.

- What time of day is your session? Consider whether food should be provided (of course, we always think food/snacks should be provided).

Creating an Agenda

You should plan your PD session with care. As you create your agenda, think of it as a lesson plan. We suggest considering the following:

- Apply what you know about how people learn and your own experience as a PD attendee as you think about pacing, movement, and engaging your participants.

- Start with the innovation adoption goals to create PD session goals. This will keep you focused on outcomes not on activities or tools.

- Connect the innovation adoption to the iMakers. Use what you created at the end of Part II and also during the "Let's Explore and Practice" section from Chapter 12.

- Aim for a balance of listening and doing. Add time estimates for each part of the session.

- Take at least a 5-minute break every 45 minutes.

- Organize all links and resources in a web-based format for participants to easily access and revisit.

- Model effective technology use in relationship to your materials, engagement of participants, and the instructional practices
  you use.

We recommend a format that includes the following:

- Start with an icebreaker activity even if participants know each
  other. Consider using technology to get participants engaged. You
  could use a polling software to gauge participant understanding
  of the topic or their perspective about being at the PD. We often
  engage participants by focusing on something we believe will be
  entertaining and will help them get to know each other better. For
  example, what is the last picture you took on your smartphone?
  We have participants get up, find a partner, and share the picture
  by describing the context of it. The icebreaker activity should take
  no longer than 5 minutes, and its purpose should be to create positive energy.

- Share the agenda so people know what to expect and when they will
  get a break.

- Create a shared understanding of the focus for the session. For example,
  if you are focusing on communication, spend time discussing what
  this means. If you are focusing on student privacy, help everyone see
  why this is important. Make sure you relate everything back to the
  innovation adoption goals.

- Balance the time between you showing and the participants doing.
  Think about chunking the technology you show them and then let
  them decide which ones they wish to explore in more depth.

- Allow time for participants to explore new technology *and* to discuss how they can use them in the learning environment. Share the
  Contemporary Skills Software Chart (Figure 9.4) from Chapter 9. This
  will give them options of software to explore if appropriate.

- Close with a recap and an evaluation. Consider modeling the use of
  technology for exit tickets, polls, or surveys to gather evaluation data
  from participants.

- Follow up the session (the next day or a few days later) by sharing the resources with participants, asking them how they are doing with using what they learned, and reminding them you are available for support.

Implementing Professional Development

We recommend the following for a smooth PD session:

- Set up early and make sure everything works.
- Have all your links open as different tabs if you are using web-based resources.
- Start on time, even if a few people are running late.
- Stay on schedule. This might mean having to say, "let's get back to that" or "this is a great conversation, but for now let's move on and revisit this in a little while."
- Promote equitable participation. If one person is dominating, have a plan for how to refocus the group to the topic while at the same time validating that individual's concerns or needs. Be ready to say statements like "That is an important topic. Let's find out what others think about it" or "I would love to talk with you about this once everyone is doing the next activity or during our break."
- Consider yourself a participant not just the leader. Join in on the conversations, complete the tasks, and model active participation.
- Remind yourself that you were chosen to lead the session because others consider you to have expertise in the area. However, it is okay to not know answers to everything or know how to do everything. Be a learner as well.

Evaluating Professional Development

During and after your PD, you will need to have opportunities for feedback and evaluation. Let's start with feedback. You should include opportunities for feedback between attendees and between you and the attendees. Feedback is an opportunity to gain input regarding individual progress toward meeting goals. You might integrate this into having a mid-point activity during workshop time in which attendees team up and share progress with the intention of being a feedback team. Feedback team members would give and receive feedback on their progress toward meeting the session goal.

In addition to feedback, you should include an opportunity for formative evaluation of the PD session. Hattie and Zierer (2018) remind us that formative evaluation "allows the teacher to use the resulting data to improve the instructional process" (p. 5). With this in mind, it would be prudent to request the attendees at different stages of the session to give you feedback by a simple thumbs-up/thumbs-down regarding "I'm ready to move on." These types of questions will help you gauge if you are in making progress toward meeting the goals of the session.

As we mentioned earlier in a Point to Consider, effective PD should not be a one-shot occurrence. You should view your PD session as being a part of a broader sequence of sessions. Therefore, you will need to have multiple opportunities for feedback and evaluation in order to determine how your participants are doing and how to improve the PD. We suggest several ways to do this.

- At the end of the session, ask participants to write down—and share with the group or to a partner—one thing they will do tomorrow, one thing they will do this week, and one thing they will use this month or semester that will help them implement what they learned during the session.

- Conduct a follow-up Stage of Concern Questionnaire using the same one you used during the Researching Phase.

- Use an exit-ticket system asking attendees what questions they still have or what additional support they might need. This could be anonymous.

- Conduct some classroom visits after a few weeks have passed. Determine the extent to which the concepts and ideas from the PD session are being implemented. Take notes in your *PURPOSE Journal* to document this.

- Develop and disseminate a short survey asking attendees to reflect on the impact of PD attendance on their current practice. Give the survey a week or two after the session.

Research to Consider: Effective Professional Development

We have shared with you our approach as teacher educators, researchers, and professional developers to planning and implementing PD. What we have shared is a combination of lessons learned in the field and years of reading research and literature on best practice for PD. You, too, should get in the habit of reading literature to support your PD decisions. Doing so will better position you to engage in conversations about asking for commitment to funding, time, and general support of your PD plan.

We have listed four research articles to get your started with the literature. One of the articles we have shared was written by Susan Loucks-Horsley (1947–2000) who was part of the original development team for the Concerns-based Adoption Model.

Borko, H., Jacobs, J., & Koellner, K. (2010). Contemporary approaches to teacher professional development. *International Encyclopedia of Education, 7*, 548–556.

Darling-Hammond, L., Hyler, M. E., & Gardner, M. (2017). *Effective teacher professional development*. Palo Alto, CA: Learning Policy Institute. Retrieved from https://learningpolicyinstitute. org/product/effective-teacher-professional-development-report

Loucks-Horsley, S., Stiles, K. E., Mundry, S., Love, N., & Hewson, P.W. (2009). *Designing professional development for teachers of science and math* (3rd ed.). Thousand Oaks, CA: Corwin.

Yurtseven Avci, Z., & O'Dwyer, L. (2016). Effective technology professional development: A systematic review. In G. Chamblee & L. Langub (Eds.), *Proceedings of Society for Information Technology & Teacher Education International Conference* (pp. 2455–2460). Savannah, GA: Association for the Advancement of Computing in Education (AACE).

Jody's Perspective From the Trenches: My Top 12 Tips for Successful Professional Development

I've learned many strategies over my years providing PD that have helped me delivers effective professional learning. I have shared my Top 12 Tips for Success!

12. *Have a backup plan.* There have been times when I've had to go completely off-line because the Wi-Fi was down or something wasn't working properly. I had a plan for how to deliver the information without participants being online, and once the Wi-Fi was backed up, we were able to continue as usual. Obviously, you want everything to work, but be prepared for when it does not. Also, be prepared for participants not knowing their passwords. This happens often.

11. *It's okay to laugh at yourself.* We have a little cheer for when things go wrong in PD sessions that I conduct. I share this cheer at the beginning of the session. When something does go wrong, we do the cheer, we laugh, and move on. If I say something wrong, I'll make a joke about it. You don't have to be perfect, but you do want to show that you are human.

10. *It's okay to not know things.* When questions arise that you don't have answers—it is okay to admit it. It makes you human and relatable when you don't know the answer to everything. The best way to handle a situation like this is to tell your participants that you don't have that answer, and it would be great to find it together. When I first started conducting PD, I was so worried that I always had to have all the answers. Now, I know it can be a learning opportunity for everyone when I don't.

9. *Survey your participants prior to the PD.* If you are able to get a list of e-mail addresses before you hold PD, put together a quick survey to gain some information about your attendees. Ask anything you need to know to plan for a more successful learning session.

8. *Prepare devices for learning.* If you have access to your learners before your session, send out an e-mail in advance of the session asking for specific apps to be downloaded (if necessary). It will save time and potential frustration if your participants already have necessary apps installed.

7. *Have participants set goals for their learning that day.* After you've shared the agenda you created, have your participants set some learning goals for the day. As you move through the room and work one-on-one with your participants, ask about goals and help ensure that they reach them. This will help them to focus and feel successful at the end of the session.

6. *Allow time for hands-on play.* If you are teaching about a technology or instructional process, make sure to build in time for participants to actually use the technology and play around with them. It's one thing to hear about something, it's quite another to actually get involved and try something out on your own. When I planned for much less talking and much more doing, my professional learning sessions were exponentially more successful.

5. *Set goals for implementing.* As part of your wrap-up, have your participants set some goals for implementation. We mentioned in this chapter that they should set a goal for what they'll do today, tomorrow, and next week to implement. Have them post this in a Google Doc or in your learning management system so that you can follow-up with them.

4. *Conduct an exit survey.* At the end of your session, ask how you did by providing a brief exit survey geared toward the learning goals of that particular session. Use a Likert scale for some questions, but also ask questions that might be hard for you to hear the answers to. It will help you grow.

3. *Play music.* Set the mood for the day by playing music as people come in to your room. Ask participants if they want music while they experiment with the technology. Sometimes people want a quiet atmosphere, but more often than not, they want background music. Be prepared with two safe-for-work playlists—one with lyrics and one that's instrumental.

2. *Bring treats.* People love homemade treats. They also love chocolate. It helps make your professional learning session feel "homey."

And the number one tip for leading successful PD is ...

1. *Have fun!* Keep the mood light, laugh, crack jokes, maybe do some singing if you are so inclined (especially if your session is after school or if you've asked people to make sub-plans to come learn with you). People learn through play. Having fun can make an event memorable.

Let's Explore and Practice!

- Locate someone you can mentor. Add a section to your *PURPOSE Journal* for documenting how this mentoring relationship progresses.

- Consider starting a two-way journal with your mentee to document what takes place. This can include sharing questions, ideas, struggles, and successes.

- Organize a "field trip" to take educators to see how others are implementing an innovation.

- Organize a "kickoff' event for the year-long PD sessions. Use this event to get individuals excited about the innovation.

- Create a potential list of PD topics. Send out a survey to gauge interest in the topics. Use this information to create your PD calendar.

- Create a flyer of the PD calendar and get participants signed up for your first three sessions.

16 | Phase Five: Operationalizing

Your role as a change age shifts during the Operationalizing Phase. Up to now, most of the work you have been involved with has mostly "behind the scenes." You were more than likely involved in completing tasks from a top-down change agent perspective rather than from a bottom-up change agent perspective. It is now time for you to be more visible to those who are being asked to change and adopt the innovation.

We can expect that some elements that we have been involved with during the previous phases have changed. The budget may have changed. Perhaps, new teachers joined the staff. Maybe some have begun using the innovation. As a result, you will need to continually revisit the steps conducted during the Understanding, Researching, and Preparing phases. While completing the steps of the Operationalizing Phase, you should have your primary goal of sustaining the innovation (the next phase in the PURPOSE Framework).

The Operationalizing Phase could be considered the implementation phase of the change process. Fullan (2016, p. 12) describes implementation as "what happens in practice," but also acknowledges that "planned change attempts rarely succeed as intended." Rogers (2003) describes implementation as the time when an "individual puts the new idea into use" (p. 169). Hall and Hord (2020, p. 14) remind us that increased support will lead to increased potential for implementation success—something that is pivotal for Operationalizing. It is important to also consider that during Operationalizing individuals are going to adopt the innovation at different rates and use it in different ways.

PHASE FIVE: OPERATIONALIZING

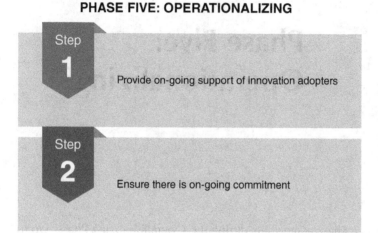

Figure 16.1 Step five of the PURPOSE framework: Operationalizing

Steps of the Operationalizing Phase

There are two steps involved in the Operationalizing phase of the PURPOSE Framework. The first step includes providing on-going support in the form of providing differentiated professional learning through professional development opportunities (e.g., mentoring, small group, whole group, online). In order to conduct the most appropriate on-going professional development, you will engage in one-legged interviews, visit classrooms, and begin to strategically document all the ways the innovation is being used. During Operationalizing, the second step will be to ensure that there is continued buy-in for the innovation adoption. These two steps go hand-in-hand. Figure 16.1 outlines the two steps and the questions associated with these steps that you should answer as you work through this phase.

Steps to Follow in Operationalizing

Providing On-going Support

During the Preparing Phase, we recommended that you develop an academic year professional development calendar. Now is the time to put that plan into action. As we noted in the Preparing Phase, often the hardest part about planning and implementing professional development is actually getting individuals to attend. That said, there are ways to overcome this:

- Consider having a badging system for professional development attendance. Discuss this with your administration and offer incentives for attending a certain number of sessions.
- Connect professional development attendance to earning technology for attendance or the completion of integrating technology or instructional practices (or both) into the classroom.
- Focus on small-group or online sessions for on-going support.
- Include opportunities for individual mentoring at all professional learning sessions.

In Chapter 4, Jody shared how she applies a gentle breeze approach to support teachers during the innovation adoption process (if you missed this, we recommend you go back and read it) From her experiences in the trenches, we learned that the best approaches to supporting innovation adopters during the Operationalizing Phase are often the informal ones. Jody shared how she implemented a very strategic professional development plan prior to operationalizing, but once the innovation was implemented, she found that a better approach was to make classroom visits, offer to model or co-teach lessons, and engage in informal conversations.

 Jody's Perspective From the Trenches: Modeling and Co-Teaching as Part of a Coaching Model

Modeling lessons has been a key component of my coaching repertoire. In the beginning of our 1:1 implementation, I was called on to come in and teach a specific app to students. This did not lend itself very well to a true coaching cycle of teaching, reflecting, adjusting, and reteaching, but it did allow me to build relationships and trust with teachers. Teachers have become more comfortable with the devices and the apps, and now I am able to do more co-teaching and modeling of instructional strategies versus teaching how to use a specific app. Make no mistake—these requests still occur, and I am still modeling tools in some classrooms. However, as we move further along in our implementation, I am able to ask questions about integration, provide ideas, and ask to co-teach to provide support as teachers try new instructional practices. Using One-Legged Interviews has helped tremendously in opening conversations about technology integration and opening doors for me to get into classrooms.

Point to Consider: One-Legged Interviews

We introduced you to one-legged interviews in Chapter 4. One-legged interviews is a name Hall and Hord (2020) use for the brief conversations that occur "between a change facilitator and an implementer about the use of the innovation" (p. 112). They add that "these opportunities are critical opportunities to address Stages of Concern. The quantity of innovation-related one-legged interviews is a strong indicator of the final degree of implementation success" (p. 112). One-legged interviews allow you, the change agent, to gauge interest in the innovation and its adoption, as well as to remind adopters of your role in supporting innovation adoption.

One-legged interviews generally start with asking "how's it going?" types of questions. At times, you may need to read between the lines, but more often than not you will be able to gauge excitement or anxiety about the innovation and innovation adoption from these responses and gestures. As a change agent, use these moments to celebrate an individual's successes and to immediately calm anxieties by offering a quick tip or by offering to come to the classroom to provide one-on-one support.

Research to Consider: Coaching Model for Professional Development

There is an abundance of research and other literature highlighting the benefits and challenges of applying a coaching model as a form of on-going professional development. Some of the benefits discussed in the literature include the following:

- Added sense of collaboration
- Increased reflective practice
- Shift in locus of control for professional development
- Power of observation on learning

Of course, there are also challenges associated with the coaching model.

- Restrictions based on time constraints and coach and teacher schedules.
- Overcoming fear or hesitation to invite the coach into the classroom.

You can read more about coaching as a form of on-going professional development in any of these resources.

Jau, L. (2013). Peer coaching as a model for professional development in the elementary mathematics context: Challenges, needs and rewards. *Policy Futures in Education, 11*(3), 290–298. Retrieved from https://journals.sagepub.com/doi/pdf/10.2304/pfie.2013.11.3.290

Liew, W. Y. (2016). Peer coaching for improvement of teaching and learning. *Journal of Interdisciplinary Research in Education, 6*(1), 64–70. Retrieved from https://university2.taylors.edu.my/jire/downloads/vol6_05.pdf

Rhodes, C., & Beneicke, S. (2002). Coaching, mentoring, and peer-networking: Challenges for the management of teacher professional development in schools. *Journal of In-Service Education, 28*(2), 297–310. Retrieved from https://www.tandfonline.com/doi/pdf/10.1080/13674580200200184

Ensuring continual commitment could be considered the end-goal of providing on-going support. Ensuring commitment, however, extends beyond those adopting the innovation. It includes other stakeholders such as parents, the community, and the school administration (or those who might be considered a source of change). There are several ways to ensure on-going commitment.

- Provide regular (weekly or monthly) reports to stakeholders about the successes. These can be small victories or larger success. The report could be as simple as announcements features in school newsletters, an e-mail, or posts on social media.

- Readminister surveys and share the results about changed concerns and perspectives about the innovation and innovation adoption process.

- Hold a showcase event in which educators and learners can share how innovation adoption has impacted teaching and learning.

- Invite and support educators to present at regional or local conferences to continue to build their confidence. Consider how this could build educator self-efficacy (think back to this discussion in Chapter 7).

- Arrange school tours for parents and community members to see implementation and impact of the innovation adoption.

 Jody's Perspective From the Trenches: Showcases and Social Media

We planned our first Technology Showcase in our second full year of implementation. We put out a call for applications, but I also asked specific teachers who I knew were implementing technology in student-centered ways to participate. We promoted the showcase through our schools and our social media channels. Our first showcase included a dress rehearsal day that took place in the morning of a professional development day, which ensured a captive audience. It was powerful for teachers to see what other teachers in the district were doing with their devices. They made connections with former students as they shared what they had learned, and they were able to go back and implement those same tools and projects in their own classrooms. The showcase has since been renamed the Student Showcase and there is no longer a dress rehearsal. We continue to host it every year in the spring. Each year, we grow by at least two new booths, and there is a mixture of teachers who have participated in the past and those that will participate for the first time. We promote the showcase throughout the year on our social media channels, and I continue to invite teachers to apply who I know are using technology in ways that others in the community and district need to hear. There is a raffle for participating teachers, and each student participant receives a certificate of participation and a tee shirt so that every participating student is wearing the same shirt. It looks great in the room and makes our students feel special. Teaches receive a swag bag of technology-based district paraphernalia that can be used in the classroom with students. It is a great deal of work to put on this show, but it is worth it to see the pride the students have for themselves and their learning.

Point to Consider: Conference Presentations

Presenting at a conference is an effective way to give teachers a platform to share their experiences and for personal on-going professional development. A good starting place is small conferences such as local affiliates of ISTE (International Society for Technology in Education). In California, we have an organization called CUE. Tim (as board member) and Jody (as a trainer and presenter) are actively involved in this organization. Regional and statewide CUE conferences are held annually. In addition to CUE, local education agencies such as the State Department of Education, District Offices of Education, and University Colleges of Education also hold small conferences for teachers to present at or attend.

We have a few tips to share about presenting at a conference.

- Submit a proposal and present with a peer. This can help ease fears associated with presenting along. This can also provide for multiple perspectives and varied experiences to be shared in one presentation.

- If you do present, remind yourself that attendees are in your session because they chose to be there. They want to learn from you—not critique you.

- Use your best teaching or professional development strategies to keep attendees actively engaged.

- Provide a link to a digital handout of the presentation.

- Encourage conversation on the topic so you too can glean new ideas and tips.

- Connect with as many educators as possible to build your professional learning network.

Let's Explore and Practice!

- Create and share a flyer of up-coming professional development opportunities.

- Connect two individuals and support them in submitting a conference proposal.

- Form a committee including educators, site administrator, parent, community member, and student to plan a learner showcase event.

- Add a section to your PURPOSE Journal to document your observations from classroom visits. If you created a digital journal, add photos and videos as well.

Phase Six: Sustaining

Rogers (2003) defines sustainability as "the degree to which an innovation continues to be used over time" (p. 183). He adds that, "unless an innovation is highly compatible with client's needs and resources, and unless clients feel so involved with the innovation that they regard it as 'theirs' it will not be continued over the long term" (p. 376). These ideas are echoed by Hall and Hord (2020), who suggest that in the United States not enough effort is put into the sustainability of innovation adoption. Hall and Hord indicate that "sustaining change requires additional time, interventions and leadership" (p. 24). The primary goal of the Sustaining Phase is to ensure that individuals continue using the innovation over a long period of time.

Steps of the Sustaining Phase

The Sustaining and Operationalizing phases go hand-in-hand. The four steps for the Sustaining Phase are similar to those of the Operationalizing Phase. The primary difference is that in the Sustaining Phase you are reflecting on and applying knowledge gained from the Operationalizing Phase. You will continue to support innovation adopters through professional development and coaching. You will continue to promote on-going commitment by encouraging other individuals to be a spokespeople for the change that is occurring as a result of the innovation being adopted. The final step of the Sustaining Phase is to revisit the entire PURPOSE Framework completed thus far, and to be able to describe the current state of the innovation adoption. This will be important because it will provide you with necessary data and documentation for the final phase of the PURPOSE Framework—Evaluating (Figure 17.1).

PHASE SIX: SUSTAINING

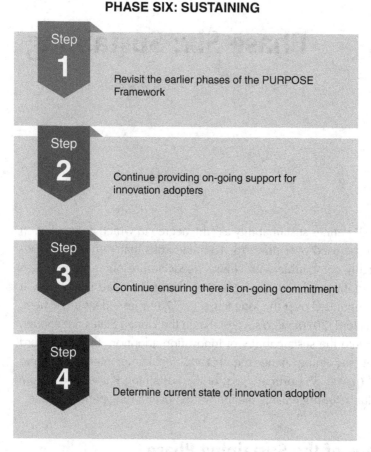

Figure 17.1 Step six of the PURPOSE framework: Sustaining

Revisiting the PURPOSE Framework Phases

It is during this step of Sustaining Phase that the recursive nature of the PURPOSE Framework is most useful. During this step, you should revisit and revise elements that from each phase of the PURPOSE Framework. Let's take a look at elements you should revisit and possibly revise.

- **Planning**
  - Revisit and if possible revise the description of what the innovation will look like when adopted.
  - Review the goals for innovation adoption.

- Revisit funding opportunities and ensure you are meeting reporting requirements for funds received.
- **Understanding**
  - Revisit and determine current perceptions of the innovation and concerns about innovation adoption.
- **Researching**
  - Check-in on Poisonous Mushrooms and determine if there are new Intervention Mushroom clusters (poisonous and nutritious) that need attention.
  - Re-evaluate sources of concerns.
- **Preparing**
  - Review whether individuals have the equipment needed to adopt the innovation or continue with the innovation adoption; determine new needs.
  - Revisit and revise your role in professional development and generating excitement about the innovation adoption.
- **Operationalizing**
  - Revisit the professional development calendar, and revise based on one-legged interviews and mentoring and coaching experiences.
  - Revisit and organize your observation notes from visiting classrooms.

Continuing On-going Support and Commitment

Operationalizing and sustaining form their own complex web within innovation adoption. We descried that the goal of the different steps and activities completed during the Operationalizing Phase is to sustain the innovation adoption. These activities if completed with consistency will ensure sustainability of the innovation adoption. During the Operationalizing Phase, you completed two steps—providing on-going support and ensuring on-going commitment. During the Sustaining Phase, you will continue to complete these same steps and associated activities, but you should be very purposeful in documenting what you are observing and planning, as well as documenting who is involved and any impact you may be observing. This is essential for completing step 4 in the Sustaining Phase.

 Point to Consider: Professional Learning Communities

Professional Learning Communities (PLCs) are common in PK-12 educational environments as a way to provide on-going support for educational practice. There are three main tenets for successful PLC adoption and implementation according to DuFour (2004). First, a mindset that all students can learn is needed of all participants. Second, DuFour (2004) suggests that PLC participants understand the power of a collaborative culture on student learning; the third tenet of a PLC, as discussed by DuFour (2004), relates to the mindset of focusing on results. DuFour suggests that the success of a PLC is evidenced in student learning outcomes. Hall and Hord (2020, p. 206) help us understand PLCs as part of Sustaining Phase by suggesting that effective PLCs must include supportive conditions and supportive leadership.

DuFour, R. (2004). What is a Professional Learning Community? Retrieved from http://www.ascd.org/publications/education-al-leadership/may04/vol61/num08/What-Is-a-Professional-Learning-Community%C2%A2.aspx

---

 ## Determining the Current State of Innovation Adoption

In order to be in a position to evaluate and reflect on the innovation adoption, it is very important that you have a clear sense of how the innovation is being adopted (i.e., what it looks like). Additionally, you will also need to have a clear sense of perceptions individuals have about the innovation if you are to determine its impact.

There are several tasks you can do to determine the current state of innovation adoption. Think of these activities as helping you create a visual representation of the innovation adoption:

- Document the progress toward reaching the goals of the innovation adoption. During this phase you are not evaluating the goals, but are simply documenting any action items that were completed and noting benchmarks that were met. Consider this to be descriptive and reflective rather than data-driven.

- If you completed the "Let's Explore and Practice" exercises from Chapter 13, you sent out a one-item survey asking individuals how they felt about the innovation. Send that same survey again. Additionally, if you sent the questionnaire asking about concerns, readminister this as well. The data you gather will provide insight into how individuals feel about the innovation.

- Complete more follow-up on how individuals are applying what they learned during professional development sessions. It is time to check in with participants and document the progress toward meeting the professional development plan goals.

- Organize your notes from mentoring, from classroom visits, and coaching. What patterns do you observe?

 ## Jody's Perspective From the Trenches: Sustaining the Innovation

As we mentioned in the beginning of this book, our initial innovation of 1:1 mobile devices in the classroom has become diffused. Three of our grade levels have 1:1 device configurations that include students taking devices home. Additionally, we have one school that has provided 1:1 take-home devices to every grade level, K-6. The Transitional-Kindergarten (TK) students at this school have 1:1 devices in their classroom. Another school has purchased 1:1 devices for each student, but the devices remain on campus. Other schools have different levels of access, but we are at a point where we have at least one device for every two students. However, just because the devices are in classrooms and in the hands of students doesn't mean that they are being used in meaningful ways across the entire district. In order to sustain this innovation, I continue to conduct needs assessments with teachers to determine professional development topics and models. I started a program called the Learner Engagement Fellowship, where teachers commit to writing and sharing technology-rich lessons based on their grade-level standards with a focus on the ISTE Standards and Universal Design for Learning. A different team of teachers is working through a model that includes co-learning, planning, co-teaching, observing, and reflecting together as a school team. The coaching that I am now able to do looks quite different from when I first started as a teacher on special assignment (TOSA). If you are in the beginning stages of your innovation and it seems like it will never be where you want it to be, take heart. Change is a long process, but your efforts will most definitely pay off.

Research to Consider: Sustaining Innovation Adoption Through a Culture of Innovation

In Part II of this book, we introduced you to our approach for understanding the *how* of educational change and innovation adoption. We shared the research of Zhao and Frank (2003) that serves as the lens through which we explore teaching and learning environments. More specific to your *how* and subsequent *what* of being a change agent is to consider the role of innovation adoption in your teaching and learning ecology. We believe that for innovation adoption and change to be sustained, they must be part of a culture of innovation. Hall and Hord (2020) describe the importance of a culture of continuous learning. A starting place to learn more about the impact of a culture of innovation on innovation adoption sustainability is with the following articles:

Herro, D. (2015). Sustainable innovations: Bringing digital media and emerging technologies to the classroom. *Theory into Practice*, *54*(2), 117–127.

Serduykov, P. (2017). Innovation in education: What works, what doesn't and what to do about it. *Journal of Research in Innovative Teaching and Learning*, *10*(1), 4–33. Retrieved from https://www.emerald.com/insight/content/doi/10.1108/JRIT-10-2016-0007/full/html

Zhao, Y., & Frank, K. A. (2003). Factors affecting technology uses in schools: An ecological perspective. *American Educational Research Journal*, *40*(4), 807–840.

Zhao, Y., Pugh K., Sheldon, S., & Byers, J. L. (2002). Conditions for classroom technology innovations. *Teachers College Record*, *104*(3), 482–515.

Let's Explore and Practice!

- Create a presentation that captures the different ways the innovation has been adopted. Use images, quotes, and if possible video vignettes. Share this presentation with stakeholders.

- Add to your PURPOSE Journal. Create a table that shows initial and follow-up data from the adopter categories and the concerns surveys you administered.

- Revisit the Planning Professional Development table you created during the Preparing Phase. Add a column titled Evidence and add data to this column.

- If your school or district does not have a Professional Learning Approach to promote a culture of continuous learning, read the research on this area and propose it as an approach to sustaining innovation adoption.

18 Phase Seven: Evaluating

Change agents understand the importance of evaluation. Evaluation provides insight into how successful our learners are. Through evaluation, we are also able to reflect on our own effectiveness. Hattie and Zierer (2018) discuss this notion. They suggest that we must reflect on the impact that our actions have on our learners, but at the same time use learner achievement and learner feedback to assess our own impact. This notion is the foundation for the Evaluating Phase. As change agents, it is important that we evaluate the impact the innovation adoption has on learner achievement and outcomes *and* use this information to evaluate our own effectiveness as a change agent.

Steps of the Evaluating Phase

There are two steps in the Evaluating Phase. First, you evaluate the impact of the innovation adoption on leaning outcomes and school goals. To do this, you will examine data collected during the Sustaining Phase. The second step is where you apply Hattie and Zierer's notion of using learner achievement and outcomes to assess your own impact. You will use the learner outcome data to reflect on the quality of the innovation adoption (Figure 18.1).

The first step in the Evaluating Phase is to **evaluate the impact of the innovation adoption**. As an educator, you should have a clear understanding of the relationship between goals, implementation, and evaluation. In order to evaluate the impact of innovation adoption, you first need to consider three questions. By answering these three questions and carefully examining the structured list you create as part of the second question, you should be able to state with a high degree the extent with which innovation adoption

PHASE SEVEN: EVALUATING

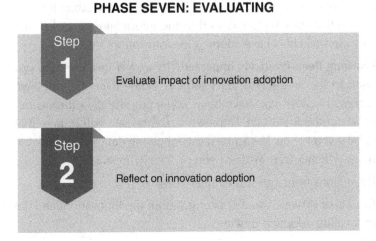

Figure 18.1 Step seven of the PURPOSE framework: Evaluating

has impacted learning. You will notice that you not only use assessment data to make this determination, but other sources of data are also used.

- **How Is The Innovation Being Implemented?** Fullan (2016) indicates that our vision for innovation adoption may not be the same as the vision of those who actually adopt it. Similarly, Hall and Hord (2020) tell us that we must start any evaluation of innovation adoption by describing the innovation adoption in action. This is the premise of their Innovation Configuration (IC) Map construct of CBAM (Concerns-Based Adoption Model). The creation of an IC Map is complex and not easily accomplished without training on CBAM and on qualitative research methodology—particularly Spradley's (1980) Domain Analysis construct. However, in your PURPOSE Journal, you have documented the different ways teachers have adopted the innovation in their classrooms. Revisit this information and look for trends in innovation use. Perhaps several teachers are using the innovation in the same way. One approach to determining how the innovation is being implemented is to conduct observations of learner and educator use of the innovation. This can provide insight into how the innovation is being implemented. Having this insight is helping in determining if the innovation adoption has been successful.

- **Examine How the Innovation Adoption Helps Meet Goals.** During Phase Six: Sustaining, you revisited the Professional Development

Planning Table you created by adding examples to the table. It's now time to use that information as well as the information regarding the different ways teachers have adopted the innovation.

- **Has Learning Been Positively Impacted?** To answer this question, you will want to use a variety of data sources. Some data you will have easy access because you have been collecting the data throughout the phases of the PURPOSE Framework. Other data will require that access be given to you. We suggest the following data to help provide insight on whether learning has been positively impacted.

  - Reflections from one-legged interviews

  - Results of surveys about concerns, about the innovation, and the innovation adoption process

  - Educator

  - Learner and educator testimonials from observations you have conducted

  - Your observations from a learner technology showcase (if you have held one)

  - Learner assessment data most likely provided by the individual who asked you to be involved or lead the change process and the innovation adoption

The second step in Evaluating is to reflect on the overall innovation adoption.

- **Start With Learning.** Doing this allows you to apply Hattie and Zierer's (2018) mind-frame of using student learning to assess your own impact. You start with this because this information can help you identify any gaps in the innovation adoption process that may need to be addressed. When you completed the first step in the Evaluating Phase, you were able to make an informed judgement about whether learning was improved as a result of innovation being adopted. Ask yourself these questions to decide if you feel the innovation adoption was successful.

  - To what extent has learning improved (or not) when data from test scores are analyzed?

  - What were the reactions of learners regarding their learning and the innovation?

- How different was learning when I looked at the different configurations of educators adopted the innovation?

- What skills and dispositions were gained as a result of innovation adoption that might not be represented in the assessment data?

- **Examine Teacher Perceptions and Concerns.** Both Fullan (2016) and Hall and Hord (2020) indicate that to see change in behavior we must first see change in perception and attitude. During the Sustaining Phase, you readministered both the concerns questionnaire and the one-item adopter category survey. Look carefully at this data. How is it different from the data you gathered during the initial and midpoint administration of the questionnaire and survey? We hope you can see a shift toward individuals feeling more comfortable with the innovation and having concerns that would represent a shift away from Unconcerned or Informational and more toward Collaboration and Refocusing. This would indicate a positive impact of the innovation adoption. Static or reverse trends would indicate the innovation adoption still has a way to go if we are to be able to consider it successful.

- **Consider the SAMR Model.** In Chapter 9, we discussed how the SAMR Model can be used to reflect on how technology is being integrated into teaching and learning. Using the descriptions of the different ways the innovation has been adopted, you can reflect on how these align to the different layers of the SAMR Model. If the different ways the innovation is being adopted align mostly with the substitution and augmentation levels, this is an indication that the adoption of the innovation has most likely not had a high level of impact on learning.

Final Thoughts: Reflecting on Innovation Adoption

As a change agent going through the change process, you have been purposeful in facilitating change and documenting the impact that resulted. Let's take some time to reflect on what took place.

- **What Worked?** Be honest with yourself. Consider your individual actions as well as larger scale events associated with the innovation adoption. Document what you felt went well.

- **What Did Not Work?** Once again, be honest with yourself. Consider your individual actions as well as larger scale events associated with the innovation adoption. Document what you felt did not work?

- **What Should Be Done Differently Next Time?** Be specific. Be thorough. This information can be used in informing the first step of your next innovation adoption process.

Key Points From Part III: The What of Educational Change and Innovation Adoption

Let's Review!

- You are a change agent who has applied the PURPOSE Framework to facilitate change and the adoption of an innovation. (All of Part III)

- Careful and procedural planning in which goals are articulated is a necessary step in innovation adoption. (Chapter 12)

- It is important that all stakeholders, including the change agent understand the change process, innovation adoption, and the innovation being adopted. (Chapter 13)

- Identification of influencers (positive and negative) can greatly impact the success of innovation adoption. (Chapter 14)

- Differentiated and on-going professional development is integral to sustained innovation adoption. (Chapter 15.)

- Individuals need support throughout innovation adoption. (Chapter 16)

- The PURPOSE Framework is highly recursive and all phases inform each other. (Chapter 17)

- Evaluation should include two level—evaluating the impact of the innovation on learning and evaluating your impact as a change agent. (Chapter 18)

Let's Explore and Practice

Now that you've made it through Part III, it is time to explore and practice with the concepts we included. We have provided a few activities that can help you delve into the concepts as well as revisit Parts I and II.

1. Each part of this book covered a different element of Simon Sinek's Golden Circle. How would you explain Simon Sinek's Golden Circle to a colleague who is not familiar with this idea? How would you use your *why*, *how*, and *what* as examples to explain the Golden Circle? Locate someone you can share this idea with.

2. You created a PURPOSE Journal as you read through Part III. Throughout Part III, we offered suggestions on what to include in your journal, but we did not prescribe how to organize it. Spend some time to organize your journal with the goal of sharing your story with others so they, too, can be inspired to live their passion.

3. You have completed a huge undertaking by being a change agent for innovation adoption in your educational ecosystem. Celebrate your accomplishments by paying it forward and helping others define their *why*, *how*, and *what*.

4. You should be feeling confident about your knowledge and skills at being a change agent. Reflect on the areas that you feel you need to continue to grow. Develop a plan to continue to improve your knowledge and skills as a change agent.

References

Anderson, M., & Jiang, J. (2018). Teens, social media & technology 2018. *Pew Research Center*. Retrieved from https://www.pewresearch.org/internet/2018/05/31/teens-social-media-technology-2018/

Australian Ministerial Council on Education, Employment, Training, and Youth Affairs. (2005). *Contemporary learning: Learning in an online world*. Retrieved from http://www.curriculum.edu.au/verve/_resources/Contemp_Learning_Final.pdf

Bandura, A. (1977). Self-efficacy: Toward a unifying theory of behavioral change. *Psychological Review, 84*(2), 191–215.

Bandura, A. (1986). Fearful expectations and avoidant actions as coeffects of perceived self-inefficacy. *American Psychologist, 41*(12), 1389–1391.

Bandura, A. (1992). Exercise of personal agency through the self-efficacy mechanism. In R. Schwarzer (Ed.), *Self-efficacy: Thought control of action* (pp. 355–394). Washington, DC: Hemisphere.

Bandura, A. (1997). *Self efficacy: The exercise of control*. New York, NY: W. H. Freeman and Company.

Battelle for Kids. (2019). *Framework and resources*. Retrieved from http://www.battelleforkids.org/networks/p21/frameworks-resources

Bennett, B. (2018). Critique: What effect size doesn't tell us. In G. E. Hall, L. F. Quinn, & D. M. Gollnick (Eds.), *The Wiley handbook of teaching and learning* (pp. 431–444). Hoboken, NJ: Wiley Blackwell.

Bennett, S., & Maton, K. (2010). Beyond the "digital natives" debate: Towards a more nuanced understanding of students' technology experiences. *Journal of Computer Assisted Learning, 26*(5), 321–331.

Brown, A., & Green, T. (2014). *Securing the connected classroom: Technology planning to keep students safe*. Eugene, OR: ISTE.

Brown, A., & Green. T. (2018). Issues and trends in instructional technology: Consistent growth in online learning, digital content, and the use of mobile technologies. In R. M. Branch, H. Lee, & S. S. Tseng (Eds.), *Educational media and technology yearbook* (Vol. 41, pp. 3–12, 61–71). New York, NY: Springer Press.

Brown, A., & Green. T. (2019). Issues and trends in instructional technology: Access to mobile technologies, digital content, and online learning opportunities continues as spending on IT remains steady. In R. M. Branch, H. Lee, & S. S. Tseng (Eds.), *Educational media and technology yearbook* (Vol. 42, pp. 3–12). New York, NY: Springer Press.

Brown, C., & Czerniewicz, L. (2010). Debunking the "digital native": Beyond digital apartheid, towards digital democracy. *Journal of Computer Assisted Learning, 26*(5), 357–369.

Buck Institute for Education. (2016). What is PBL? Retrieved from http://bie.org/about

Carpenter, J., & Green, T. (2018). Self-directed professional learning and educator self-efficacy: The case of Voxer. In C. B. Hodges (Ed.), *Self-Efficacy in instructional technology contexts*. New York, NY: Springer.

CAST, Inc. (2019). *About universal design for learning*. Retrieved from http://www.cast.org/our-work/about-udl.htm

Centre for Teaching and Excellence. (n.d.). *Gamification and game-based learning*. Retrieved from https://uwaterloo.ca/centre-for-teaching-excellence/teaching-resources/teaching-tips/educational-technologies/all/gamification-and-game-based-learning

Christensen Institute. (2016). *Blended learning*. Retrieved from http://www.christenseninstitute.org/blended-learning/

Clifford, M. (2012). *Bring your own device (BYOD): 10 reasons why it's a good idea*. Retrieved from https://www.opencolleges.edu.au/informed/other/bring-your-own-device-byod-10-reasons-why-its-a-good-idea/

Coe, R. (2002). *It's the effect size, stupid: What effect size is and why it is important*. Paper presented at the Annual Conference of the British Educational Research Association, University of Exeter, England. Retrieved from https://www.leeds.ac.uk/educol/documents/00002182.htm

Cristol, D., & Gimbert, B. (2013). *Academic achievement in BYOD classrooms*. 12th World Conference on Mobile and Contextual Learning (mLearn 2013) (Vol. 15). Retrieved from http://www.qscience.com/doi/abs/10.5339/qproc.2013.mlearn.15

Culatta, R. (2009). *Categorization of learning technologies*. Retrieved from http://innovativelearning.com/instructional_technology/categories.html

Delgado, A. J., Wardlow, L., McKnight, K., & O'Malley, K. (2015). Educational technology: A review of the integration, resources, and effectiveness of technology in K-12 classrooms. *Journal of Information Technology Education, 14*, 397–416.

Dimock, M. (2019). Defining generations: Where millennials end and generation Z begins. *Pew Research Center*. Retrieved from https://www.pewresearch.org/fact-tank/2019/01/17/where-millennials-end-and-generation-z-begins/

Donohoo, J. (2017). *Collective self-efficacy: How educators beliefs impact student learning* (1st ed.). Thousand Oaks, CA: Corwin, Sage.

Donovan, L., & Green, T. (2010). One-to-one computing in teacher education: Faculty concerns and implications for teacher educators. *Journal of Digital Learning in Teacher Education, 26*(4), 140–148.

Donovan, L., & Green, T. (2014). *Making change: Creating 21st century teaching and learning environments*. Huntington Beach, CA: Shell Education.

Donovan, L., Green, T., & Hartley, K. (2010). An examination of one-to-one computing in the middle school: Does increased access bring about increased student engagement? *Journal of Educational Computing Research, 42*(4), 423–441.

Donovan, L., Green, T., & Mason, C. (2014). Examining the 21st century classroom: Developing an innovation configuration map. *Journal of Educational Computing Research, 50*(2), 161–178.

Education Superhighway. (2019). *2019 state of the states report*. Retrieved from https://stateofthestates.educationsuperhighway.org/

Engle, G., & Green, T. (2011). Cell phones in the classroom: Are we dialing up disaster? *TechTrends, 55*(2), 39–45.

Ertmer, P. A. (1999). Addressing first-and second-order barriers to change: Strategies for technology integration. *Educational Technology Research and Development, 47*(4), 47–61.

Ertmer, P. A. (2005). Teacher pedagogical beliefs: The final frontier in our quest for technology integration? *Educational Technology Research and Development, 53*(4), 25–39.

Evans, J. (2019). *Digital learning: Peril or promise for our k-12 students.* Retrieved from https://tomorrow.org/Speakup/downloads/2018_19-Speak-Up-National-Congressional-Briefing-Paper.pdf

Evergreen Education Group. (2019). *Snapshot 2019: A review of K-12 online, blended, and digital learning.* Retrieved from https://www.evergreenedgroup.com/keeping-pace-reports

Facer, K., & Furlong, R. (2001). Beyond the myth of the "Cyberkid": Young people at the margins of the information revolution. *Journal of Youth Studies, 4*(4), 451–469.

Flipped Learning Network (FLN). (2014). *The four pillars of F-L-I-P™.* Retrieved from http://www.flippedlearning.org/definition

Florida Center for Instructional Technology. (n.d.). *The technology integration matrix.* Retrieved from https://fcit.usf.edu/matrix/matrix/

Fullan, M. (2007). *The new meaning of educational change* (4th ed.). New York, NY: Teachers College Press.

Fullan, M. (2013). *Stratosphere: Integrating technology, pedagogy, and change knowledge.* Don Mills, ON: Pearson Canada, Inc.

Fullan, M. (2016). *The new meaning of educational change* (5th ed.). New York, NY: Teachers College Press.

Gartner. (2019). *Gartner hype cycle.* Retrieved from https://www.gartner.com/en/research/methodologies/gartner-hype-cycle

Green, T., & Brown, A. (2018). *The educators guide to producing new media open educational resources.* New York, NY: Routledge.

Green, T. D., & Donovan, L. (2018). Learning anytime, anywhere through technology. In G. E. Hall, L. F. Quinn, & D. M. Gollnick (Eds.), *The Wiley handbook of teaching and learning* (pp. 225–256). Hoboken, NJ: John Wiley & Sons.

Hall, G. E., & Hord, S. M. (2020). *Implementing change: Patterns, principles, and potholes* (5th ed.). Hoboken, NJ: Pearson.

Halverson, E., & Sheridan, K. (2014). The maker movement in education. *Harvard Education Review, 84*(4), 495–504.

Hatch, M. (2014). *The maker movement manifesto*. New York, NY: McGraw-Hill Education.

Hattie, J. (2009). *Visible learning*. New York, NY: Routledge.

Hattie, J. (2012). *Visible learning for teachers*. New York, NY: Routledge.

Hattie, J., & Zierer, K. (2018). *10 Mindframes for visible learning: Teaching for success*. New York, NY: Routledge.

Helsper, E., & Eynon, R. (2010). Digital natives: Where is the evidence? *British Educational Research Journal*, *36*(3), 503–520.

Hewlett Foundation. (2016). *Open educational resources*. Retrieved from http://www.hewlett.org/programs/education/open-educational-resources

International Society for Technology in Education (ISTE). (2019a). *ISTE standards*. Retrieved from https://www.iste.org/standards

International Society for Technology in Education (ISTE). (2019b). *ISTE standards for coaches*. Retrieved from https://www.iste.org/standards/for-coaches

Istance, D., & Paniagua, A. (2019). *Learning to leapfrog: Innovative pedagogies to transform education*. Washington, DC: Center for Universal Education at Brookings Institute.

Januszewski, A., & Molenda, M. (Eds.). (2008). *Educational technology: A definition with commentary*. London, England: Routledge.

Keller, G., & Passan, J. (2013). *The one thing: The surprisingly simple truth behind extraordinary results*. Austin, TX: Bard Press.

Kennedy, G., Judd, T., Dalgarnot, B., & Waycott, J. (2010). Beyond natives and immigrants: Exploring types of net generation students. *Journal of Computer Assisted Learning*, *26*, 332–343.

Kolb, L. (2011). *Triple e framework*. Retrieved from https://www.tripleeframework.com/about.html

Koutropoulos, A. (2011). Digital natives: 10 years after. *Journal of Online Learning and Teaching*, *7*(4). Retrieved from http://jolt.merlot.org/vol7no4/koutropoulos_1211.htm

Lee, J. J., & Hammer, J. (2011). Gamification in education: What, how, why bother? *Academic Exchange Quarterly*, *15*(2), 1–4.

Margarayn, A., Littlejohn, A., & Vojt, G. (2011). Are digital natives a myth or reality? University students' use of digital technologies. *Computers in Education*, *56*(2), 429–440.

Martin, L. (2015). The promise of the maker movement for education. *Journal of Pre-College Engineering Education Research (J-PEER)*, *5*(1), 30–39.

Means, B., Blando, J., Olson, K., Middleton, T., Morocco, C., Remz, A. R., & Zorfass, J. (1993). *Using technology to support education reform*. Washington, DC: Department of Education, Office of Education Research and Improvement.

Mell, P., & Grance, T. (2011). *The NIST Definition of Cloud Computing*. National Institute of Science and Technology, Special Publication, 800-145, 1–7.

Miller, A. (2019). *3 Myths of personalized learning*. Retrieved from https://www.edutopia.org/article/3-myths-personalized-learning

Murphy, R., Snow, E., Mislevy, J., Gallagher, L., Krumm, A., & Wei, X. (2014). *Blended learning report*. West Lake Hills, TX: Michael & Susan Dell Foundation. Retrieved from https://www.edweek.org/media/msdf-blended-learning-report-may-2014.pdf

National Science Board. (2018). *Science and engineering indicators 2018*. NSB-2018-1. Retrieved from https://nsf.gov/statistics/2018/nsb20181/report/sections/elementary-and-secondary-mathematics-and-science-education/references

Oblinger, D. G., & Oblinger, J. L. (2005). *Educating the net generation*. Washington, DC: EDUCAUSE. Retrieved from https://net.educause.edu/ir/library/pdf/pub7101.pdf

OECD. (2011). *The second digital divide*. Retrieved from http://oecdinsights.org/2011/06/28/reading-the-second-digital-divide/

Papert, S., & Harel, I. (1991). *Constructionism*. Retrieved from http://www.papert.org/articles/SituatingConstructionism.html

Parsons, D., & Adhikari, J. (2016). Bring your own device to secondary school: The perceptions of teachers, students and parents. *The Electronic Journal of e-Learning*, *14*(1), 66–80. Retrieved from http://davidparsons.ac.nz/papers/ejel-volume14-issue1-article486.pdf

Prensky, M. (2001). Digital natives, digital immigrants part 1. *On the Horizon*, *9*(5), 1–6.

Project Tomorrow. (2011). *Learning in the 21st century: 2011 trends update*. Retrieved from https://tomorrow.org/speakup/learning21Report_2011_Update.html

Project Tomorrow. (2018a). *Mobile learning snapshot: How students use mobile devices for learning, June 2018*. Retrieved from https://tomorrow.org/speakup/speakup-2017-how-students-use-mobile-devices-for-learning-june2018.html

Project Tomorrow. (2018b). *Speak Up research initiative, 2017-18 findings*. Retrieved from https://tomorrow.org/speakup/speakup_data_findings.html

Project Tomorrow. (2019). *Millennial, Gen X and Boomer parents: Leveraging mobile-enabled social media for school-to-home communications across the generations*. Retrieved from https://tomorrow.org/speakup/millenial-gen-x-and-boomer-parents-report-2019.html

Reinhart, J. M., Thomas, E., &; Toriskie, J. M. (2011). K-12 teachers: Technology use and the second-level digital divide. *Journal of Instructional Psychology, 38*(3/4), 181–193.

Rideout, V. J., Foehr, U. G., & Roberts, D. F. (2010). Generation M 2: Media in the Lives of 8- to 18-Year-Olds. Henry J. Kaiser Family Foundation. https://eric.ed.gov/?id=ED527859

Robinson, L., Brown, A., & Green, T. (2010). *Security vs. access: Balancing safety and productivity in the digital school*. Eugene, OR: ISTE.

Rogers, E. (2003). *Diffusion of innovation* (5th ed.). New York, NY: Free Press.

Rose, D. H., & Meyer, A. (2002). *Teaching every student in the digital age: Universal design for learning*. Alexandria, VA: ASCD.

Rosen, L. D., Carrier, L. M., & Cheever, N. A. (2010). *Rewired: Understanding the iGeneration and the way they learn* (Kindle ed.). New York, NY: St. Martin's Press.

Seels, B. B., & Richey, R. C. (2012). *Instructional technology: The definition and domains of the field*. Bloomington, IN: Association for Educational Communications and Technology.

Seemiller, C., & Grace, M. (2018). *Generation z: A century in the making*. London, England: Routledge.

Sharples, M., McAndrew, P., Weller, M., Ferguson, R., Fitzgerald, E., Hirst, T., & Gaved, M. (2013). *Innovating pedagogy 2013: Open University innovation report 2*. Milton Keynes, England: The Open University.

Sinek, S. (2009). *Start with why: How great leaders inspire everyone to take action*. New York City, NY: Penguin Group.

Spradley, J. P. (1980). *Participant observation*. Belmont, CA: Wadsworth Cengage.

Strauss, W., & Howe, N. (2000). *Millennials rising: The next great generation*. New York, NY: Vintage Books.

Tapscott, D. (1999). *Growing up digital: The rise of the net generation*. Boston, MA: McGraw-Hill.

Tapscott, D. (2009). *Grown up digital: How the net generation is changing your world*. Boston, MA: McGraw-Hill.

Trilling, B., & Fadel, C. (2009). *21st century skills: Learning for life in our times*. Hoboken, NJ: John Wiley and Sons.

Tschannen-Moran, M., & Barr, M. (2004). Fostering student learning: The relationship of collective teacher efficacy and student achievement. *Leadership and Policy in Schools, 3*(3), 189–209.

Twenge, J. M. (2018). *iGen: Why today's super-connected kids are growing up less rebellious*. New York, NY: Atria Books.

U.S. Office of Education, Office of Educational Technology. (2016). *Future read learning: Reimagining the role of technology in education*. Retrieved from http://tech.ed.go/file/2015/12/NETP16.pdf

White, K. R. (1982). The relation between socioeconomic status and academic achievement. *Psychological Bulletin, 91*, 461–481.

Zhao, Y., & Frank, K. A. (2003). Factors affecting technology uses in schools: An ecological perspective. *American Educational Research Journal, 40*(4), 807–840.